The Bible

and

Farm Animal Welfare

The Bible

and

Farm Animal Welfare

DAVID GRUMETT

CASCADE *Books* • Eugene, Oregon

Cascade Books
An Imprint of Wipf and Stock Publishers
199 W. 8th Ave., Suite 3
Eugene, OR 97401

www.wipfandstock.com

PAPERBACK ISBN: 979-8-3852-1859-2
HARDCOVER ISBN: 979-8-3852-1860-8
EBOOK ISBN: 979-8-3852-1861-5

Cataloguing-in-Publication data:

Names: Grumett, David [author].

Title: The Bible and farm animal welfare / David Grumett.

Description: Eugene, OR: Cascade Books, 2024 | Includes bibliographical refer-
ences and index.

Identifiers: ISBN 979-8-3852-1859-2 (paperback) | ISBN 979-8-3852-1860-8
(hardcover) | ISBN 979-8-3852-1861-5 (ebook)

Subjects: LCSH: Animals in the Bible. | Animal rights—Religious aspects—
Christianity. | Domestic animals. | Animal welfare. | Human–animal relation-
ships.

Classification: BT746 G78 2024 (paperback) | BT746 (ebook)

VERSION NUMBER 062824

For Peter Jinman (1951–2023)
veterinary surgeon, leader, raconteur

Contents

Acknowledgments | ix

Introduction | 1

1. Herds and Flocks | 6

2. Bodies | 30

3. Behavior | 52

4. Stockpersons | 68

Epilogue | 90

Bibliography | 93
Scriptural Index | 105
Subject Index | 109

Acknowledgments

I AM GRATEFUL TO many colleagues and collaborators who have deepened my understanding of farm animal welfare and offered encouragement of different kinds. These include Donald Broom, Andy Butterworth, Madeleine Campbell, Pen Rashbass, Kate Rigby, Sarah Wolfensohn, and Steve Wootton. Peter Atkins kindly read and commented on a draft of the manuscript. Robin Parry guided the project and also provided valuable comments on the text. I am also indebted to countless farmers, stockpersons, and farm workers who have welcomed groups that I have been part of onto farms to learn about what goes on day by day, usually out of public view.

This book was made possible by an Arts and Humanities Research Council grant (AH/R014752/1) for a project on the Christian ethics of farm animal welfare with David Clough and Siobhan Mullan.

Introduction

BECAUSE BIBLICAL SOCIETIES WERE agricultural, it is unsurprising that farm animals feature prominently in biblical myth, narrative, parables, and imagery. As nomadic and herder lifestyles came to be replaced by settled living, many households occupied small-holdings on which humans lived alongside animals, relying on them for food, fibre, fertilizer, transport, and income. The ongoing closeness of animals to humans probably had the effect of making them somewhat invisible: we sometimes fail to observe, or to reflect on, that with which we are most familiar. Because animals are not referred to in a particular biblical passage, this does not mean that they have no place in what is being described. For example, ruminant animals are likely to have remained close to a well and would often have been the reason why humans were standing at a well conversing. They are likely to have been inside, or close to, the accommodation in which Jesus was born, even though the canonical Gospels make no reference to them there.[1]

It would be easy to infer that, because animal herding and farming were, in biblical societies, largely outdoor and small scale, husbandry should be of a similar type and scale today. However, current animal farming needs to be assessed against modern expectations about methods and welfare standards. It cannot be assumed that the animals that were farmed in biblical settings experienced either higher or lower welfare than those that are farmed today in a variety of indoor and outdoor systems. Animals farmed

1. Luke 2:6; Matt 2:11.

1

in economically developed countries are likely to enjoy a reliable supply of food and water, and protection from disease, predation, and adverse weather conditions. In biblical settings, in contrast, many farm animals died from illness, predators were a constant threat, against which shepherds were only partly effective, and the provision of food and water could not be assured.[2]

In the course of this book, I will show that a biblical understanding of farm animals may aid the consideration of their welfare in several ways. For both Christians and non-Christians, viewing these animals in husbandry systems that were extensive and unmechanized encourages a renewed focus on the animals themselves, including their biological needs and normal behaviors, rather than on animals as products and as sources of products. For non-Christians, understanding how the husbandry systems and practices described, and sometimes mandated, in the Bible had the effect of promoting good welfare may help to disabuse them of the well-worn yet unfounded notion that Christianity is anthropocentric and is therefore bad news for animals. For Christians, such understanding is likely to motivate a concern for the welfare of the animals that supply their meat, eggs, and milk today. The Bible not only informs fundamental theological doctrines about God and the moral principles governing the treatment of humans but has implications for the non-human sentient world.

Humans are both like and unlike different farm animal species. As with farmed mammals, but unlike in chickens and geese, human embryonic development occurs within the womb rather than inside an egg that has been laid and is then incubated. We are dissimilar to any farmed species, especially pigs and chickens, in normally producing only one offspring at a time. Our production of single offspring is also because, unlike any farmed species, we are altricial, that is, we are highly dependent, following birth, and for an extended time period, on adult care, while our physical capacities and advanced mental functioning develop. Similarly to pigs and chickens, we are monogastric, ingesting food and digesting it in a stomach comprised of a single chamber. This contrasts

2. Exod 9:3; Ezek 34:3, 5, 8.

with the four stomach chambers of ruminant animals, which enable them to consume grass and other plants. Like greylag geese, but unlike the major farmed species, we are normally monogamous. Pairings are formed that endure over an extended time period, providing a setting for the rearing of successive young. Like farmed species in general, we are gregarious, living in extended families and in social groupings.

In biblical societies, as today, most animals were farmed in order to be slaughtered so that meat could be produced for human consumption. Until the development of modern stunning technologies during the nineteenth century, killing an animal by cutting its neck and allowing its blood to drain out was the quickest and least painful method available.[3] This method was also theologically significant, because the blood of both animals and humans was seen as representing their life force, with exsanguination marking the boundary between life and death.[4] In slaughterhouses today, bleeding out an animal as quickly as possible remains a key stage in the slaughter process.

In this book, I use the term "farm animals" to designate animals that have been bred for farming and are farmed. As a result of ongoing husbandry over many generations, these animals have developed distinctive characteristics and needs. In focusing on farm animals, I do not wish to suggest that animals that live in other kinds of relationship with humans, such as companion animals and entertainment animals, are unimportant. Farm animals are the subject of this book because of the deep dependence upon them that humans have developed, the extremely large scale of animal farming, and the ubiquity of farm animals in biblical texts. Moreover, although the same animal species may be both farmed and wild, this book is not directly concerned with wild animals, apart from where discussion of them, such as their individual and group behavior, illuminates understanding of farm animals. Humans do not have the same duty of care to wild animals as they do to animals under their control.

3. Fairholme and Pain, *A Century*, 173–90.
4. Gen 9:4–5; Carmichael, "On Separating Life and Death."

The book is arranged in four chapters. The first presents farm animals in the group setting that is natural to them. These groups are frequently large, even in the wild, and are highly structured according to age, sex, physical characteristics, and tradition. Herdmates and flockmates interact for both procreation and companionship, exhibiting characteristic behaviors. For females, nesting, giving birth, and providing maternal care to young are significant life activities that they are strongly motivated to perform. The second chapter turns to farm animal bodies. Male farm animals that have not been castrated help to bring females into fertility and procreate with them to produce young. Several other body parts aid living and allow animals to express normal behaviors, with the importance of different parts varying between species. Tails protect from the elements, aid balance, indicate mental state, and may be used to remove insects from body skin and hair. Horns indicate social rank, may be deployed defensively and offensively, and aid thermoregulation. Among piglets, birth teeth help to increase the survival chances of smaller littermates, and, for all pigs, snouts are intrinsic to rooting. Similarly, beaks enable chickens to feed and groom. This chapter ends with a consideration of how intentional breeding may either promote welfare or undermine it, and a reflection on lifespan.

The topic of the third chapter is behavior. The possibilities available are, in large part, a function of habitat and ground substrate, with outdoor rearing potentially providing extensive roaming and browsing opportunities. Ingesting and digesting food are shown to occupy a large portion of the waking day. Fish and chickens possess highly sophisticated navigational abilities, and play is important in the physical growth and socialization of young. The book's final chapter concerns stockpersons. The humans who care for farm animals are set apart from those animals and closely determine their lives. Yet they also live alongside these animals, performing roles that would otherwise be fulfilled by herdmates or flockmates, such as guarding and parenting. The role of the stockperson is decisive for welfare, is largely out of public view, and requires dedication and commitment. The human–animal bond is such that animals will sometimes perceive stockpersons as one of their own. Despite the changing role of the stockperson, and the increasing use of technology for husbandry purposes, a farm remains a single community comprised of both farm animals and humans.

1

Herds and Flocks

FARM ANIMAL SPECIES HAVE strong and stable group identities. For easy husbandry, and to achieve a high scale of production for meat and secondary products such as milk and eggs, the species that have been selected and bred for farming comprise individuals that are content to live alongside each other. Domesticated ruminants graze and move as a group, with individuals learning from herdmates and group tradition. For these species, group identity more strongly determines association than maternal bonds or kin affinity. Females provide a herd structure in which age seniority is more significant than physical characteristics.

The strong group identity of farmed species is recognized in the Bible. Animals are normally represented collectively, as part of a herd or a flock. The group identity of farm animal species displays to humans the social life that they should themselves lead. By means of ongoing observation and habituation, farmers and shepherds working in the societies that are described in the Bible were deeply attuned to the group dynamics of domesticated species. Today, in settings where farming systems alter natural animal groupings, these dynamics are less visible. However, wild, feral, and extensively free-ranging groups provide important information about species behavior when constraints imposed by humans are minimal or absent.

In Christian theology and church tradition, the group identity of humans is similarly fundamental. Believer identity derives from membership of a church or other faith community, rather than being defined by an internalized faith, or by a self-selected set of outward practices such as worship or diet. This church or community is prefigured by God's election of a whole people, Israel, as chosen. Moreover, a classic view of salvation is that this also is collective, with the salvation of individuals dependent on the final gathering together and saving of the entire human species.[1] In modern Roman Catholic social teaching, the collective perspective prioritizes the pursuit of the common good for all above the provision of individual goods for a privileged few.

In this chapter the group and intergenerational dynamics of farm animal species will be examined. I shall first consider the natural group dynamics of domesticated species, especially sheep, examining how these are presented in the Bible as examples of organization and behavior that human groups should observe and from which they may learn. I shall then examine sexual interaction and attachment, which are necessary for any animal group to continue over time, showing how the sexual behavior of farm animals is part of their individual and group identity. In the final section, I shall address gestation, nesting, birth, and maternal care, explaining how these are particularly important for the dams (mothers) and young of some farmed species.

1. Group Identity, Structure, and Tradition

Animals as signs

The first systematic theological account of how and why animal behavior is instructive for Christians is developed by Augustine of

1. Lubac, *Catholicism*, 217–45.

Hippo as part of his theory of signs. The early fifth-century bishop, who ministered in North Africa, developed Plato's distinction between things and signs, recognizing animals—among them cattle and fish—to be givers of signs.[2] Whereas a thing is objectified by human rational categories and use, a sign exceeds such categorization, pointing beyond itself and thus giving new knowledge and meaning. Moreover, Augustine held that, because of the tremendous importance of the Bible for Christian knowledge and life, animals that appear in it, such as farm animals, have special significance.

In the lineage of animal signification that descended from Augustine, there was a tension between attending to animals that lived in and around human communities, and so were easily observable, and reflecting on those in habitats that were distant from human communities, but which possessed characteristics that supported particular points of moral or theological instruction. Within the *Physiologus*, which was a bestiary that widely circulated during the medieval period, numerous wild animals, and even some mythical beasts, appear, but no major farmed species is found. Given that farm animal species live close to humans and are prominent in the Bible, it is surprising that medieval theologians did not generally follow Augustine's lead in recognizing them to be sign givers. Such recognition requires that these species not be viewed merely in terms of the human needs and wants that they might satisfy and how well they fit into human farming systems. Rather, as created beings that reveal something of the order and goodness of the world, farm animal species may reveal truths to humans that have relevance in their own lives.

Animal groups

In the Bible, the language used to describe domesticated species is typically collective. Seven pairs of the species classified as clean

---

2. Augustine, *De doctrina Christiana* 2 III 4 (4) and XVI 24 (59–60), 58–59, 82–85. For further discussion, see Grumett, "Animals," 582–85.

enter the ark of Noah, not just one.[3] Abraham keeps flocks (*tson*) of sheep and goats as well as herds (*baqar*) of cattle, with the large size of his holdings indicating his prosperity and status.[4] In the Song of Songs, a flock (*eder*) of goats descending from the mountains is used to image the hair of the beloved.[5] At Jesus's birth, the shepherds to whom the angel appears are watching over a flock (*poimne*) of sheep that was probably combined with goats.[6] When Jesus encounters two demon-possessed men, the pigs close by are feeding in a herd (*agele*).[7] The fact that the Hebrew *tson* and the Greek *poimne* both designate a mixed group of sheep and goats indicates that these small ruminants were frequently grazed together, as is explicitly stated of the flocks of Laban and in the prophecy of Ezekiel against Israel.[8] The two species sometimes needed to be separated for husbandry purposes, such as milking. Matthew's Gospel builds on Ezekiel's imagery by vividly associating this separation with God's judgment of the righteous and of sinners.[9]

On the rare occasions when live domesticated animals are depicted as individuals, they are typically in distressing situations. For instance, in Nathan's parable to David, the incident of the rich man with large flocks seizing the poor man's only ewe lamb (*kibsah*) to prepare as a meal for his guest appears all the more shocking because the poor man's lamb is taken and slaughtered alone.[10] In Matthew's Gospel, in a parable told by Jesus, the plight of the sheep (*probaton*) that falls into the pit on the sabbath is intensified because it is solitary.[11]

3. Gen 7:2a.
4. Gen 12:16; 13:5; 18:7; 20:14; 21:27.
5. Song 6:5.
6. Luke 2:8.
7. Matt 8:30–32; Mark 5:11–13; Luke 8:32–33.
8. Gen 30:32; Ezek 34:17. See Lincoln, "Translating," 322–26.
9. Matt 25:32–33.
10. 2 Sam 12:1–4.
11. Matt 12:11.

Sheep

Although the Bible presents several domesticated species, sheep (*probata*) are the most common and the most prominent. Human groups are repeatedly compared with a flock of sheep. In Matthew's Gospel, Jesus favorably portrays the Israelites, to whom he sends the apostles, as sheep. Later in this gospel, in teaching on the second coming, the sheep represent those people who are blessed and who inherit the kingdom.[12] In John's Gospel, at the recommissioning of Peter on the lakeside, Jesus presents his followers as lambs and sheep.[13] In the letter to the Hebrews, in a passage on which Easter worship blessings are sometimes based, the people led by Jesus are identified as both lambs (*arnia*) and sheep.[14] These comparisons of humans to sheep are fitting because a flock of sheep and a group of humans exhibit similarities in composition and dynamics. A neutral or favorable comparison suggests that, in the view of the author, narrator, or speaker, there are flock characteristics that stockpersons and other humans should respect and from which they might learn.

What are these characteristics? Sheep are sociable, and for protection while grazing keep together and orient themselves so that other flock members, with whom they communicate through posture and movement, remain within their field of vision. Notwithstanding variations by individual personality, a study of a flock of Scottish Blackface sheep found that they grazed on average eight meters apart.[15] When on the move, sheep travel as a flock. Among wild and feral flocks in hilly and mountainous regions, traditions that are passed down through generations enable knowledge to be preserved of steep or rocky terrain across which animals may escape predators, and of migratory routes to shelter and forage in different seasons. The fourth-century bishop and theologian Basil of Caesarea recognizes this capacity of flocks to

---

12. Matt 10:5–6; 25:32–34.
13. John 21:15–17.
14. Heb 13:20; e.g., *Common Worship*, 317.
15. Sibbald et al., "Individual Personality."

find their own way under the guidance of lead animals, which can be either ewes or rams. Reflecting on the Vulgate translation of the opening of Psalm 29, "Bring to the LORD the offspring of rams," he writes: "The ram is an animal capable of leading, one which guides the sheep to nourishing pastures and refreshing waters, and back again to the pens and farmhouses." Using the ram as an image for a church leader, Basil continues:

> Such are those who are set over the flock of Christ, since they lead them forth to the flowery and fragrant nourishment of spiritual doctrine, water them with living water, the gift of the Spirit, raise them up and nourish them to produce fruit, but guide them to rest and to safety from those who lay snares for them. . . . If the leaders of the rest are the rams, their children would be those formed to a life of virtue through zeal for good works by the teaching of the leaders.[16]

It is notable that Basil does not view the flock as requiring a human shepherd. Rather, it has a self-organizing capacity based on structure and inherited learning. In a population of wild bighorn sheep observed in Alberta, a related feature of group organization, which confirms the importance of tradition, was the consistency with which individual rams chose, over successive years, to remain within the flock during the mating season or to leave.[17] This suggests a stable understanding by individuals of their place in the group and of annually recurring events.

Flock continuity is provided by ewes, who rarely depart during the mating season. Among the Alberta bighorn ewes, there was a dominance hierarchy strongly correlated with age. Unlike in ram groups, physical characteristics such as horn size were less significant in determining individual status. Because dominance was age related, individuals did not achieve an elevated hierarchical position until later in life; however, elderly ewes were supplanted. Reproductive success in one generation did not increase the

---

16. Basil of Caesarea, "A Psalm of David" 2, 195. Ps 29:1: "Adferte Domino filii Dei, adferte Domino filios arietum."

17. Festa-Bianchet, "The Social System," 76.

chances of success in the next generation: 64 percent of ewes aged between five and six years had surviving dams, but there were only three known grandmother–granddaughter pairs among forty-five ewes.[18] High status was not inherited.

Referring to the feeding behavior of young lambs, Basil states that God their creator "compensated for the deficiency of reason by the superiority of their senses." He continues:

> Really, how is it that among countless sheep a lamb, leaping out from the fold, knows the appearance and voice of its mother, hurries toward her, and seeks its own source of milk? Even if it finds the maternal udder dry, it is satisfied with it, running past many that are heavy with milk. And how does the mother know her own among the countless lambs? They have one voice, the same appearance, a like odor among all, as much as reaches our sense of smell, but, nevertheless, they have a certain sense impression that is keener than our perception, through which the recognition of its own offspring is possible for each animal.[19]

Basil thus correctly records the well-testified ability of pre-weaned lambs to seek out and identify their dams. Bishop Ambrose of Milan offers similar observations, acknowledging this even within very large herds and describing the dam's corresponding capacity to identify her own young.[20] However, from about six months of age, when weaning is completed, these dam–lamb pairings diminish. Beyond weaning, the Alberta bighorn ram lambs remained within larger ewe groups until joining the spring congregation at two years of age, or occasionally at one year of age. Most then returned to these groups, not forming their own until after the third or fourth congregation. However, neither ram lambs nor ewe lambs maintained any close association with their own dam.[21] Similar detachment from the dam after weaning has been observed

18. Festa-Bianchet, "The Social System," 74–75.

19. Basil, "On the Hexameron" 9.4, 142.

20. Ambrose, *Hexameron* 9.4 (25), 243–44.

21. Festa-Bianchet, "The Social System," 78–79.

in free-ranging Scottish Blackface lambs.[22] Although ewe lambs continued to be found in the vicinity of their dams, this was due to peer association immediately following maternal separation, and then to mixed-age group association, and was not accompanied by preferential interaction with their own dam. Similar patterns of association, including home ranges focused on ewe groups, have been observed among the Soay sheep on the Scottish archipelago of St Kilda, from which the last remaining native human inhabitants departed in 1930.[23]

Despite their strong flock solidarity, sheep are hospitable to newcomers. Among the Alberta bighorns, two or three flocks were observed sharing a range for grazing with no hostility, even though they remained within their own group as a result of possessing the ability to identify flockmates from that group.[24] In this study, flock size varied widely, from five up to seventy adult ewes. However, flocks may be much larger, with over one thousand sheep common in modern settings. Jesus refers to this tendency of sheep flocks to welcome new members, and thus to increase in size, when stating that, in addition to the sheep that are currently of his fold (*aule*), there are other sheep not currently of it that must also be brought in.[25] The behavior of sheep flocks is thus instructive for his followers, as they establish their own groups and, through example and mission, these increase in size.

In summary, sheep are highly social animals that flock, observe, and communicate well. These behaviors are primarily for protection from external threats. Tradition informs the decisions of groups and individuals. Ewes provide flock stability and form an age-related hierarchy, although do not maintain maternal bonds with their own young beyond weaning. In contrast, rams may spend periods outside the flock, and their hierarchy is more

22. Lawrence, "Mother, Daughter and Peer Relationships."

23. Grubb, "Social Organization."

24. Festa-Bianchet, "Seasonal Dispersion."

25. John 10:16. The term *aule* describes an enclosed but unroofed space. Its Latin derivative *aula* is frequently used to describe the assembly hall of a seminary or university.

dependent on physical characteristics. Sheep flocks are welcoming to newcomers and may peaceably combine.

Cattle

The group composition and dynamics of other farm animal species now need to be considered. Unlike for sheep, the Bible does not present the group aspects of these other species in detail. Nevertheless, now that we have established the principle that group composition and dynamics is biblically important, this issue may be examined by using research in animal behavior.

The behavior of cattle herds is similar to that of sheep flocks in several key aspects. Herd solidarity is due to females and the composition of subgroups is comparable. For instance, a study of feral cattle on Amsterdam Island in the Pacific Ocean, which were left following the departure of French settlers in 1871, found three kinds of group: (i) all-age females, and males up to three years old; (ii) males from a year of age, living and grazing at upper altitudes for most of the year; and (iii) mixed-sex groups constituted in advance of the breeding season by the assimilation of males into the all-age female group. The mean average group size was eleven for females and younger males, but a much lower 3.5 for all-male groups, which included many isolated individuals.[26] However, cattle herds can be less fluid than sheep flocks, with a stable hierarchy promoting coexistence within closed herds. During observation of the much-studied white Chillingham herd, which has survived in Northumberland in England since medieval times, no extended agonistic behavior was observed.[27] Among a group of semi-wild Scottish Highland cattle in a German nature park that was studied over four years, which included uncastrated males, a stable and clearly defined hierarchy was preserved that incorporated both cows and bulls.[28] Factors determining rank within the hierarchy

26. Daycard, "Structure Sociale."

27. Hall, "Chillingham Cattle." For background, Whitehead, *The Ancient White Cattle.*

28. Reinhardt et al., "Social Behaviour."

included assertiveness, age, and sex. A younger male was able to be dominant over an older female although no female was in a dominance relation over an older male.

Among the Chillingham cattle, there are far more males than in a closely managed herd, which leads to potentially greater competition for mating success in year-round breeding, and no males are castrated. Yet bull fencing bouts (i.e., any horn-to-horn contact) mostly occur between members of the same home range group.[29] This suggests that such bouts are a means of maintaining an existing group hierarchy, rather than a consequence of bullying or distress. The cattle on Swona, which have been feral since the Scottish island's last human inhabitants withdrew in 1974, have been observed to forage in a single group in winter and to maintain a hierarchy among mature bulls. During a six-day observation period, a brown bull that remained close to the main herd was seen to assert dominance over two other brown bulls, which kept a greater distance.[30] Two younger and smaller black bulls maintained a closer association with the main herd, while another mature black bull remained further away at the north end of the island.

It might be assumed that a closed and stable herd would suffer genetic disadvantage due to inbreeding. However, in cattle, the inbreeding that results from a closed herd does not necessarily entail diminished fertility or group health. Within the Chillingham herd, a pronounced lack of genetic variation has not led to lethal recessive mutations. This is because the polymorphic loci that are present are dispersed in clusters along the genome at chromosomal locations that are probably key to genetic fitness, rather than being evenly distributed.[31] This genetic evidence, combined with behavioral observation, suggests that cattle have a greater need than sheep to live in a stable group, including the freedom to choose how closely to relate to the group.

29. Hall, "Chillingham Cattle," 224–25.
30. Hall and Moore, "Feral Cattle."
31. Williams et al., "Inbreeding and Purging."

Chickens

Chickens are not clearly referred to in the Old Testament and were probably not farmed for their meat or eggs in this period.[32] However, chicken is today the land species farmed in by far the greatest numbers worldwide, as well as being the most hierarchical farmed species. A seven-year study at San Diego Zoo tracked birds through their lifetime. It confirmed the existence of a comprehensive pecking order between cocks, with just one peck by one bird of another bird reliably indicating relative status within the flock, which remained within a very tightly delimited geographical area close to other flocks.[33] Status would only be reordered by fighting. Moreover, during their period of supremacy, dominant cocks enjoyed far higher reproductive success than their subordinates, being responsible for as many as 60 percent of the matings observed in the central flock. A few hens were seen to mate with other cocks, from either their own flock or a neighboring flock, while hiding out of view. Even so, the reproductive success of hens was similarly uneven, with just four out of twenty-eight of these hens rearing one half of the total chicks to independence.[34] Eleven hens did not raise any chicks to independence. The most reproductively successful hens lived for approximately three years on average, but these others lived for only about two years. This strong and finely graded hierarchy sharply contrasts with what is found among sheep and cattle, although the closed nature of the group has similarities with cattle.

32. MacDonald, *What Did the Ancient Israelites Eat?*, 36–37. In the New Testament, a cockerel is, of course, prominent in the Passion narrative, when its vocalization confirms Peter's denial of Jesus (Matt 26:34, 74b; Mark 14:30, 72; Luke 22:34, 60–62; John 13:38; 18:27). This is consistent with the suggestion that chickens were introduced into the region by the occupying Roman forces.

33. Collias and Collias, "Social Organization."

34. Collias et al., "Dominant Red Junglefowl."

Pigs

In the Bible, pigs receive little attention because they were regarded as unclean and were therefore not widely farmed by the ancient Israelites.[35] Indeed, in the parable of the two sons, working as a swineherd in a far country represents the younger son's utter estrangement from his family, culture, and religion.[36] Unlike with sheep, pig behavior is not used to image human social interactions, even though pig groupings more closely correspond to the structure of human nuclear families. In natural settings, pigs usually remain within small groups that rarely comprise more than three adults. In a semi-natural environment in Scotland, these typically consisted of a boar, two older sows each with an adult daughter, a subadult of each sex, and any unweaned young.[37] The relationship that was established by physical proximity was reinforced by grooming. The group integration of pigs has been found to be easiest at a young age, with relatively little aggression shown when piglets from different litters mix at ages of up to four months. In one study, head knocking, shoulder-to-shoulder contact, and neck biting comprised just 17 percent of observed interactions, being far outweighed by positive explorations such as nose-to-body contact, scamper contact, nose to anal-region contact, and mounting.[38] The natural preference of pigs to live in small groupings has obvious implications for farming. Serious behavioral problems commonly arise when pigs are placed into large groups.

2. Sexual Interaction and Attachment

In the Song of Solomon, the beloved is repeatedly compared with a young stag leaping over the mountains.[39] Imagery using other undomesticated species is also deployed in this biblical book, with its

35. Borowski, *Every Living Thing*, 140–44. See also chapter 2.4.
36. Matt 21:28–32.
37. Stolba and Wood-Gush, "The Behaviour of Pigs."
38. Petersen et al., "Integration of Piglets."
39. Song 2:9, 17; 8:14.

erotic undertones suggesting that sexual drives have an important place in the created order in motivating the production of new life and thus the continuation of species. Whereas the group structure of farm animal species could be preserved without males, for reproduction, males are essential. Among ruminants, prior to the act of mating, the presence of males, even if vasectomized, increases female fertility, due to linked visual and olfactory cues, and promotes their return to fertility after a previous birth.[40] Moreover, the presence of males alongside females enables both sexes to perform normal behaviors.

As has been shown, the group identity of farm animals is presented in the Bible as a significant positive trait from which humans may learn. In contrast, from both theological and sociological perspectives, the promiscuous sexual interactions and mating of farmed species differ from commonly accepted human norms. Most farmed species mate with multiple partners, which increases the total number of matings, and therefore the number of young produced, within a given time period. Few theological sources are available to appraise the sexual interactions of farm animals. However, the form that these interactions take in different farm animal species when they are in natural settings has been studied by animal behaviorists.

Among farm animal species, one or more males identify that a female is approaching fertility, and the female indicates her preference. Within a mixed-sex herd, a bull detects a cow two days before she comes into oestrus and remains nearby "guarding" her.[41] During this period, the cow will hyper-react to external stimuli, and will approach other herd members that transgress the herd hierarchy. As oestrus is reached, the bull more closely follows the cow, mounting her, or licking and smelling her, before curling his upper lip. He often throws up dirt and may snort or rest his chin upon the cow's rump. A ram, in order to achieve proximity to a ewe in oestrus, adopts a low stretch and twist approach to her,

---

40. Martin et al., "Natural Methods," 233–35; Monje et al., "Male Effect."

41. Hafez and Bouissou, "The Behaviour," 217–26. A cow in oestrus is ready for mating.

sniffing her and her urine.[42] He may move his tongue in and out of his mouth, vocalize, or rub and bite the ewe. The ram follows her until she stands still and allows him to mount. Among pigs, sows or gilts entering oestrus become highly sensitized to external stimuli, vocalize with a soft rhythmic grunt, and seek the boar.[43] The boar then follows the female, noses her body, and emits a soft frequent grunt. The sow responds by nuzzling the boar's flanks and rear, biting his ears, and sometimes trying to mount him. The boar rubs the sow on the back and she adopts a rigid stationary stance. Among chickens, the cock seeks receptive and preferred hens, dancing, or fluttering his wings.[44] To signal receptivity, hens may crouch, according to individual preference.

In farm animal species, male–male sexual interaction is partly a function of early rearing conditions. For example, among a group of Saanen goats, bucks reared within a wholly male group were, after reaching adulthood, more likely than those that had been reared with does to mount other bucks.[45] This suggests that male–male sexual interaction is partly socialized. Among lambs, sexual interaction between males is common. In Uruguay, a group of Milschaf lambs of the same age, who were sired by the same ram and remained in contact with adult ewes through the experimental period, were observed on pasture. Until seven months of age, they exhibited progressively increasing male–male sexual interaction. This included sniffing, lateral approaches, and mounting.[46] This same-sex interaction was accompanied by increased sexual interest in ewes in oestrus. Nevertheless, approximately 8 percent of rams exhibited a consistent sexual preference for other rams. This preference appears to be linked to aspects of brain structure and chemicals.[47]

42. Fisher and Matthews, "The Social Behaviour," 225–26.

43. Signoret et al., "The Behaviour," 302–11.

44. Fischer, "The Behaviour," 469–76.

45. Ungerfeld et al., "Does Heterosexual Experience Matter?"

46. Ungerfeld et al., "Relationship."

47. Roselli et al., "The Development."

Male–male sexual interactions may be a cause for concern if, in environmental conditions appropriate to the species and breed, there is a risk that they may lead to injury. A notable instance is what has been termed "buller" syndrome, which is exhibited by some young, neutered males, including those at pasture. Certain steers allow themselves to be repeatedly mounted by others or are selected for such treatment. Some steers that are ridden are relatively large and aggressive, which suggests that they may seek this, whereas others that receive such treatment occupy a low position in the hierarchy, or are unwell.[48] Cow–cow sexual interaction, including head to rump positions and mounting, is also observable when one or both females are in oestrus.[49] Indeed, cows displaying frequent or irregular oestrus activity—which have frequently been described as nymphomaniac—may be as sexually aggressive as bulls.[50] However, any risks resulting from nonreproductive sexual interactions, whether between animals of the same sex or of opposite sexes, are likely to be offset by the benefits of these interactions in coordinating the actions of group members and their concern for the wellbeing of other individuals.[51]

As has been seen, most farmed species are promiscuous. An exception is greylag geese, which is the geese species standardly farmed in Europe and North America. The factors favouring monogamy include the settling of migrated flocks, gander assertiveness, and the timing of moulting. After returning from winter feeding areas in early spring, migratory flocks split into pairs due to increasing antagonism between ganders.[52] The minority of females that are breeding nest together in colonies but are sufficiently distanced and hidden to be invisible to each other. When laying commences, the gander leaves the nest, and the female relies for protection on camouflage, although the gander watches the nest and intervenes if a predator appears. At hatching, the

48. Blackshaw et al., "Buller Steer Syndrome."
49. Hurnik, "Sexual Behavior," 436–37.
50. Hafez and Bouissou, "The Behaviour," 224.
51. Ulishney, "The Evolution."
52. Kotrschal et al., "Making," 47–48.

gander returns to his female and goslings, and the family join a larger gaggle, with the gander continuing to provide protection, including from other geese. During this rearing period, before the goslings can fly, the adults moult and so are also unable to fly. Basil of Caesarea refers to the vigilance of geese and their keen perception of hidden dangers, and this could be what Ambrose has in mind in his description of their "nightly sentry watches" signalled by cackling.[53]

Prior to forming pair-bonds, geese engage in behaviors that may be regarded as courtship, such as remaining physically close over several weeks, walking in parallel, and other behavioral synchrony. Observers have considered a bond to have been formed once the triumph ceremony[54]—in which the courting gander makes to attack another bird, then turns around and runs toward the partner with body held high, wings flapping, and loud cackling—has been responded to by greeting behavior. The partner's neck falls parallel to the ground and is swung with vocalization. The ethologists studying semi-tame free-ranging greylag geese at Grünau in Austria comment: "One cannot help to see the analogy with a human wedding ceremony, where partners in front of witnesses confirm their bond to each other."[55] Individual pair bonds often last several years. The bonds that are constituted may be mixed sex or exclusively male, with some ganders entering into both during their lifetime. In the Grünau study, 49 percent bonded exclusively with females, 37 percent bonded with both females and males, and 14 percent bonded only with males.[56] Older ganders were more likely to pair with other males. Triads might form when a third member became attached to the dyad, but this member,

---

53. Basil, *On the Hexameron* 8.7, 130; Ambrose, *Hexameron* 8.13 (44), 197. Both refer to the account in Livy, *History of Rome* 5.47, 156–61, of this behavior alerting the Roman garrison to a surprise night attack during a siege by the Gauls, which enabled the attack to be repulsed. Despite the famine, because geese were regarded as sacred to Juno, they had not been slaughtered. The sentinels learnt from the geese to maintain a more careful watch.

54. Fischer, "Das Triumphgeschrei."

55. Kotrschal et al., "Making," 53.

56. Kotrschal et al., "Making," 54–66.

even if enjoying sexual relations with one or other member of the dyad, was usually marginal in the bond's ceremonial performance.

Among greylag geese, both male–female and male–male interaction are thus comparable with human monogamy. From a theological perspective, an ongoing relationship between two sentient beings that are capable of recognizing each other images God's covenantal love and commitment to the world and to all beings within it. The behaviors that have been described in this section suggest that the relationship's sex configuration is not a significant difference. Extraordinarily, some older animal behavior research, as well as assumptions in practical farm management, suggest that same-sex attraction—which, in farmed species, is usually male–male—is unnatural, and therefore needs to be managed or preferably eliminated. For example, a cattle research group working in the United States referred to male–male mounting by steers as a "common . . . homosexual vice."[57] In another study, male–male sexual interaction among rams was described as a "fault."[58] It is unclear why same-sex attraction is singled out for censure, when so many aspects of behavior that are considered to be natural are changed or disrupted within farming systems.

Some behavioral studies have considered same-sex animal pairings to be based on misidentification. This explanation is in principle feasible for geese and for other farmed species, because the appearance of males and females is similar. However, because female geese are no more capable of correctly identifying (whether visually, or by other means) the sex of flockmates than ganders, but do not form same-sex pairings, this account is unlikely to be correct.[59] Another hypothesis has been performative, with male-male pairings being viewed as an outcome of some males exhibiting behaviors associated with females. However, in the Grünau study, ganders were not found to perform any such behaviors when forming such pairings. Rather, male-male pairings, like male-female pairings, cemented a social alliance, enabling the maintenance and

57. Klemm et al., "Homosexual Behavior," 187.

58. Chenoweth, "Libido," 166.

59. Kotrschal et al., "Making," 66–73.

advancement of individual position within the group. A notable benefit of this included being able to forage closer to the center of the group, where food quality was likely to be higher and the risk from predators lower.

3. Gestation, Nesting, Birth, and Maternal Care

Birth

It is in relation to giving birth that farm animal species, especially females, exhibit some of their most remarkable behaviors. These illustrate the intricate and wondrous evolved design of the created order that is presented in Job, in which animals and birds are commended as the teachers of humans.[60] The writer of one of the oldest books in the Bible justly presents aspects of the gestation and birth of animal species that may be farmed as beyond full human comprehension. Close to the book's ending, God addresses Job out of the whirlwind, asking:

> Do you know when the mountain goats give birth?
> Do you observe the calving of the deer?
> Can you number the months that they fulfill,
> And do you know the time when they give birth,
> When they crouch to give birth to their offspring,
> And are delivered of their young?[61]

Although understanding of such matters is greater now than in the time of Job, some aspects remain obscure and, once known, appear remarkable. A good example is the coordination of birth. For instance, among the feral cattle in the Parque Nacional de Doñana in southwest Spain, there is a degree of synchronization. This promotes socialization, because, being born at roughly the same time, herd members are of similar ages.[62] Within a group studied

---

60. Job 12:7.
61. Job 39:1–3 (NRSV).
62. Lazo, "Social Segregation."

in South Dakota, oestrus was synchronized by females that had not yet mated undertaking olfactory exploration of other cows.[63] The resulting synchronization was increased by females with good body condition that mated after the seasonal peak, exhibiting a gestation period that was, on average, six days shorter, even though this led to their young recording bodyweights on average twenty kilograms lower at six months. The fact of group synchronization despite this physiological cost to some individuals indicates its considerable social benefits, as well as its importance in reducing predation losses.

Among a range of bird species, synchronization is due to embryos. A domesticated hen lays fertilized eggs over a period of several days and sits on different eggs for different durations. Yet hatching is more synchronized than if it were simply a function of these factors, with embryos communicating and hastening the hatching of near neighbors by producing clicking sounds at variable rates by tapping their egg tooth against the shell wall.[64] These sounds are heard by embryos in eggs that are touching their own, and possibly by others.

Nesting

Before their young are born, two farmed species naturally undertake nesting site selection and nest building. With domesticated pigs, which exhibit similar nesting behavior to wild boars, this may be divided into several stages.[65] One to three days before the time of birth, the sow selects a nesting site, preferring areas with trees or other vegetation cover. In an unusual reference to pigs, Psalm 80:13 realistically presents such a forest boundary habitat. About a day before, the sow begins building, hollowing out ground then gathering and arranging nesting material, which includes thick branches, which give the nest stability. A crucial purpose of

63. Berger, "Facilitation."

64. Tong et al., "Embryonic Development," 624; White, "Effects."

65. Wischner et al., "Nest-Building Behaviour;" Gustafsson et al., "Maternal Behaviour," 29–42.

the nest is to provide a warm environment for the piglets, which are usually born hairless and at less than 1 percent of adult body weight. In order to reduce the risk of piglet crushing, the sow defends her nesting site from other adults. If the sow rolls onto one of the piglets, the nest structure and gaps are likely to protect the piglet from serious injury.

As is well known, hens, like many other birds, also construct nests. These enable the hen to sit on top of her eggs without them rolling away or being crushed, thus providing the warmth that is essential for incubation and hatching. In the Bible, nesting in a range of locations appropriate to species is presented as a natural bird behavior.[66] Methods include gathering, in which the hen moves her litter materials closer to her body by pecking or raking with her beak or head; litter-placing, in which she picks up litter particles and throws them over her shoulder; and rotating, in which she crouches, turns on the spot, and scrapes outwards with her feet. One study suggests that the manipulation of nesting materials using the body and feet is more important to hens than manipulation by means of their beak, and that individuals develop preferences for particular nesting materials, which they consistently seek out.[67] In another study, hens performed nesting behaviors even if a nest that they had previously constructed was made available, and even if it contained one of their eggs.[68] This indicates that, as for pigs, nesting is a behavioral need for hens, as well as serving practical purposes.

Maternal Care

The writer of the Song of Songs celebrates lambing. Referring to the beloved, he enthuses: "Your teeth are like a flock of shorn ewes

66. Pss 84:3; 104:17; Isa 34:15; Jer 48:28; Matt 8:20. The ostrich practice of not constructing a nest out of gathered materials but scraping a dip in the ground is referred to in Job 39:14–15, along with the risk of crushing by another animal.

67. Duncan and Kite, "Nest Site Selection."

68. Hughes et al., "The Performance."

that have come up from the washing, all of which bear twins."[69] Lambing is thereby connected with the cleaning of the ewes that typically occurs before mating. Bishop Augustine uses this as a suggestive image for admission into the church and for the love of God and neighbor. He states: "It is with the greatest of pleasure that I visualize the shorn ewes, their worldly burdens set aside like fleeces, ascending from the pool (baptism) and all giving birth to twins (the two commandments of love)."[70] Although twin births are normal among modern sheep breeds enjoying good health and nutrition, they are much rarer among wild and feral populations and were probably similarly exceptional in fourth-century North Africa.

Once young mammals have been born, they are initially dependent on a female, who is typically their dam, for survival. Biological needs include colostrum, milk, warmth, and shelter. However, while basic physical needs are being met, aspects of normal behavior are being expressed by both the dam and her young. The importance of this initial period—during which the dam and her young remain together, maternal care is lavished, and young respond—is highlighted at several points in the Bible. God tells Moses that even a sacrificial calf or lamb must remain with its dam for a week before being offered to God.[71] This means that an animal killed at a young age has experienced direct maternal care, and that its dam has been allowed the opportunity to exercise this. Under no circumstances may an animal and its young be killed together.[72] Within the same portion of teaching, the Israelites are instructed that they must not boil a kid (*gedi*) in its mother's milk.[73] Although the implications of this requirement have been debated, in so far as it upholds the intrinsic value of the nursing of young by their dams, it potentially calls into question the slaughter

---

69. Song 4:2 (NRSV).

70. Augustine, *De doctrina Christiana* 2 VII 9 (16), 63.

71. Exod 22:30; Lev 22:27. See Murray, *The Cosmic Covenant*, 114–15.

72. Lev 22:28.

73. Exod 23:19b, also 34:26; Deut 14:21.

of all pre-weaned goats and all does in lactation.[74] Moreover, in Jewish tradition, the requirement has sometimes been expansively interpreted as applying not only to goats but to all ruminants. The effect of these injunctions is significantly to extend the duration that dams and their young must be permitted to spend together beyond that prescribed for sacrificial animals. It allows the dam to perform maternal functions, including feeding through to weaning, and leaves the young to enjoy the maternal bond through this period.

An evocative biblical image of maternal care is provided by the prophet Ezra: God reminds the Israelites that he has gathered them "as a hen gathers her chicks under her wings." Echoing these words, Jesus describes in two of the Gospels his urge to gather the children of Jerusalem around him as a hen gathers her brood beneath her wings.[75] When unfolding this image, Martin Luther, who was an Augustinian friar, draws on his own experience of hens:

> Let us observe how a natural mother-hen acts. There is hardly an animal that takes care of its offspring so meticulously. It changes its natural voice turning it into a lamenting, mourning one; it searches, scratches for food and lures the chicks to eat. When the mother-hen finds something, she does not eat it, but leaves it for the chicks; she fights seriously and calls her chicks away from the hawk; she spreads out her wings willingly and lets the chicks climb under her and all over her, for she is truly fond of them—it is, indeed, an excellent, lovely symbol.[76]

Luther compares the actions of Jesus to those of the hen teaching her chicks the skills they will need to gain early independence. He envisages chicks that have left the nest requiring protection from predators, attentive induction into foraging, and close physical contact. Confirming Luther's observations, research indicates that

74. Keel, *Das Böcklein*.

75. 2 Esd 1:30 (NRSV); Matt 23:37; Luke 13:34.

76. Martin Luther, "The Gospel for St. Stephen's Day, Matthew 23[:34–39]," translated by Hans J. Hillerbrand, in Luther, *Works*, 52.97–98.

a brooding hen indeed motivates exploration, teaching her chicks to ground peck and to perch at height.[77]

Although sows are similar to hens in their nesting behavior, they differ from hens in maternal care. Piglets observed during the first three months of life were found, throughout this period, to have stronger bonds with littermates, although not with specific littermates, than with either their dam or any other piglet.[78] Indicators of these bonds included adjacent resting, imitating behavior, close sniffing, and playful interactions such as butting. Excepting piglets up to a month old sniffing their dam and those up to three months old sniffing a wide range of other pigs and piglets, the large majority of behaviors were directed toward littermates. The mixing of litters was gradual and based on the social relationships of dams, especially dam–daughter pairs.

Among cattle, the bond between a cow and her calf is enduring. In an observational study of a herd of Salers cattle, the calves remained with their dams even after weaning, and up to and beyond the next calving. Cows suckled and licked their newborn, although during long daily periods of grazing, for which mobility is required, their year-old calf remained alongside them while the newborn rested further away.[79] This is in sharp contrast with the behavior of both domestic hens and pigs, which do not maintain a close bond.

4. Conclusion

This chapter has drawn on both biblical sources and animal behavior research to show that the group structure of farm animal species, the attachments within them, and their capacity to produce new generations, are each fundamental to their identity and flourishing. In the Bible, the dynamics of sheep and goat groups are frequently referred to, and animal behavior research confirms

77. Riber et al., "Effects."
78. Newberry and Wood-Gush, "Social Relationships."
79. Veissier et al., "Social Behaviour."

that group dynamics are, with some important differences, equally important to other farmed species. The interactions and attachments of farm animals and birds are also recognized in the Bible, with behavioral research providing detailed understanding. Giving birth, and the events that precede and follow this, are recognized in the Bible as manifestations of the wonder of creation, and even current animal behavior researchers do not fully comprehend all their aspects.

In summary, all domesticated species live as groups and have highly developed social structures. Christian theologians, including many bishops, used these as models for church organization, leadership, and mission. Group structure is maintained primarily by aged-related female hierarchy, although males have their own hierarchy, which is principally based on physical characteristics and helps to protect the group. Domesticated species display characteristic mating behaviors and, excepting geese, are promiscuous. Sexual interaction between males is common across species and is part of normal behavioral repertoire. Frequent and relatively easy births are another feature of domesticated species. These are preceded by mating behaviors and, in pigs and hens, by nesting. Newborns bond both with their dam and with kin. The duration and strength of these bonds changes with time and varies between species.

2

Bodies

FARM ANIMALS, LIKE HUMANS, use their bodies for a wide range of purposes. From a species-survival viewpoint, the most fundamental of these is reproduction. Other purposes that animal bodies fulfill include rooting, pecking, removing sources of irritation, heating and cooling, protecting other body parts, displaying social status, defense, and attack. These purposes enable individual animals, and animal groups, to continue their biological life, obtain food and water, reduce their disease vulnerability, and flourish. Animals are either born with, or subsequently develop, the bodily organs and instruments they need to make their way, alongside others, through their life.

In the Bible, a key principle is that the bodily integrity of farm animals should be respected. The removal of bodily parts in order to make husbandry tasks easier, or to provide food delicacies for humans, is consistently prohibited. This prohibition applies most obviously to sacrificial animals, which must be offered unblemished. However, the conviction on which it is based, that the bodily wholeness of animals is fundamental to their flourishing, is more widely applicable. The frequency with which the requirement to preserve bodily integrity is restated suggests that, during the Old Testament era, this was not always done. Rather, respect for bodily integrity was a farming principle that could serve as a distinguishing mark between the ancient Israelites and other peoples.

In this chapter, the significance of different bodily parts for particular species will be considered in turn. These include reproductive organs, tails, horns, piglet teeth and pig snouts, and chicken beaks. The chapter ends with a discussion of lifespan. The duration for which an animal lives determines the maximum possible use and enjoyment that it will have of its body, and the extent to which herdmates and flockmates may benefit from its care and companionship.

1. Flourishing Male Animals

In the Pentateuch, it is stated in multiple places that the animals offered for sacrifice must be *tamim*, that is, without defect or blemish. The Passover lamb is to be without defect, and, at the priestly consecration of Aaron's sons, two rams without defect are offered.[1] The bull, sheep, or goat that is offered as a burnt offering, or as a well-being sacrifice, must be without defect.[2] A priest making reparation for an unintentional sin that has brought guilt upon people must offer a bull without defect, while a ruler guilty of the unintentional transgression of a commandment must offer an unblemished male goat.[3] An ordinary person who is guilty of the unintentional transgression of a commandment must offer an unblemished female goat or sheep, and the ram presented as a guilt offering for unintentional ritual sin, or for various intentional sins against others, must be unblemished.[4] Even the two male lambs and the female lamb offered by lepers—who were typically impoverished and socially marginalized—at their cleansing must all be without defect.[5]

1. Exod 12:5; 29:1.
2. Lev 1:3, 10; 3:1, 6. On Leviticus, see Douglas, "The Forbidden Animals," 13–18; Douglas, *Purity and Danger*, 63–64.
3. Lev 4:3, 23.
4. Lev 4:28, 32; 5:15, 18; 6:6.
5. Lev 14:10.

A freewill offering or an offering to pay a vow, whether made by Israelites or resident aliens, must be a male bovine, sheep, or goat without defect.[6] At the consecration of Nazirites, the male lamb, ewe lamb, and ram that are presented as, respectively, a burnt-offering, a sin-offering, and a well-being offering must all be unblemished, while the red heifer slaughtered outside the camp, whose ashes are used to purify a person following contact with a corpse, must be unblemished.[7] The two male lambs to be offered daily, as well as the two lambs that are offered in addition on each sabbath, and the seven lambs that are offered at the start of each month, during the Passover festival, and on the first day of harvest, must all be without defect.[8] The same applies to the lambs offered on Rosh Hashanah and Yom Kippur, and to the fourteen male lambs that are offered on each of the seven days of Succoth, as well as to the seven male lambs that are offered on Simchat Torah.[9] In Deuteronomy, which focuses on social life rather than on the temple and its ritual, it is simply stated that no sheep or ox with a defect must be offered.[10]

Later in Israelite history, at the consecration of the restored temple in Jerusalem, God instructs Ezekiel to offer a sin offering of a male bull, ram, and goat, all unblemished, the day after the altar is erected, and on each of the following six days.[11] At the New Year, an unblemished bull must be offered.[12] Later in the first month, during the week of Passover, the ruler must provide seven young bulls and seven unblemished rams each day, as well as a similar offering during the week of Succoth.[13] On each sabbath day, the ruler is to offer six unblemished lambs and an unblemished ram, and, at

6. Lev 22:19.
7. Num 6:14; 19:2.
8. Num 28:3, 9, 11, 19, 27, 31.
9. Num 29:2, 8, 13, 17, 20, 23, 26, 29, 32, 35.
10. Deut 17:1.
11. Ezek 43:22–25.
12. Ezek 45:18.
13. Ezek 45:23, 25.

the new moon, a similar offering accompanied by an unblemished bull.[14]

What the requirement to offer an animal without defect or blemish precisely entailed is likely to have varied. The absence of physical injury or disease was assumed.[15] However, from a husbandry viewpoint, the *tamim* requirement prohibited the castration of male animals. Among the religions of neighboring ancient Asia Minor, reproductive capacity was similarly highly prized, and entire bulls and rams represented virility.[16] In the Old Testament context, a castrated animal is most clearly identified as defective or blemished in Leviticus 22:24–25 (NJPS): "You shall not offer to the LORD anything bruised or crushed or torn or cut . . . for they are mutilated (*mishchath*), they have a defect (*mum*)."

These sacrificial requirements influenced husbandry practices across ancient Israel. At the time of Jesus, the Passover was observed domestically as well as at the Jerusalem temple. Philo describes the whole people offering sacrifice, in commemoration of the household sacrifices that were made without priests.[17] This was due to the urgency of marking the doorposts and lintels of the houses in which the Israelites lived with the blood of a lamb, before the midnight destruction of the firstborn Egyptians, whose dwellings were identifiable by not being thus marked.[18] The Roman historian Flavius states that, around the start of the First Jewish War in 66 CE, two hundred and fifty-five thousand, six hundred lambs were sacrificed at the Passover.[19] However, it has been calculated that, over the two hours of the annual Passover sacrifice,

---

14. Ezek 46:4, 6.

15. Lev 22:22.

16. Collins, "Animals," 309–11.

17. Philo, *On the Special Laws* 2.27 (145–49), 394–97.

18. Exod 12:21–27.

19. Josephus, *The Jewish War* 6.9.3 (423–26), 300–301. The purpose of this figure is to estimate the total Israelite population. Assuming Passover gatherings of an average of ten people, which approximates to the twelve who shared the Last Supper, the Roman-Jewish historian infers this to be 2.7 million.

only eighteen thousand lambs could have been killed within the Jerusalem temple precinct.[20]

Reproduction enables animals to generate offspring and so to continue their species and genetic line. The social context in which mating occurs was discussed in chapter 1.1. There it was explained that the herd or flock structure centres on adult females, and that adult males remain at a distance for much of the year. The displays and rituals that precede mating were described in chapter 1.2. In the act of mating itself, in farmed ruminants the male then impregnates the female, who, if fertile, may produce an embryo that may gestate in the womb and may then be born. The herd fertility and welfare benefits of not physically castrating male animals of different species have been established by animal welfare research.

In livestock species, the presence of males increases and hastens female fertility. Males secrete chemicals via feces, urine, or skin glands, which are smelled by females and stimulate hormonal responses in them.[21] The males enabling this may be vasectomized by having undergone a surgical procedure to prevent semen transmission from the testicles, and therefore reproduction. However, these "teaser" animals remain physically intact, and are still able to produce testosterone and ejaculate. Running such males with females improves female fertility and enables males to express normal behavior, while retaining the herd health and management advantages of control over breeding. Alternatively, males running with the herd may not have been vasectomized, and so are also able to reproduce.

Among a herd of seventy-nine heifers in Uganda, bull exposure reduced the average age of puberty attainment by more than three months, to an average of twenty-three months.[22] In an experiment conducted in Montana, cows that were accommodated close to bulls from about two months after giving birth resumed ovular function far more quickly than cows that had been kept distant from bulls. The greatest difference was found during the first three

20. Jeremias, *Jerusalem*, 82–84.
21. Rekwot et al., "The Role."
22. Rekwot et al., "Effects."

weeks, with three times as many cows regaining fertility after one week of close contact with bulls, and twice as many cows regaining it after two and three weeks of such contact.[23] Cows that were permitted only fenceline contact with bulls also resumed ovular function more quickly than the cows that were accommodated at distance from bulls, although the difference was less significant. In New Zealand, similar differences in the age of puberty onset were observed between ewe groups with close ram contact and with no contact. Behavioral problems leading to a perceived need to isolate and castrate bulls are likely to be due to the mixing of herds, unconfident handling by stockpersons, and the simple fact of isolation from herdmates.[24] One study has produced similar findings for ewes. Their fertility after fourteen days of running with rams was double, or, for those of greater bodyweight, even quadruple, the level of fertility when the sexes were segregated, with the difference becoming less significant at twenty-eight days.[25]

Among female pigs in Britain, the presence of boars (i.e., uncastrated males) has been found to advance the attainment of puberty by roughly forty days, with the greatest effect occurring when five-and-a-half-month-old gilts were mixed with multiple boars, rather than with a single boar.[26] As with cows, the effect of fenceline contact, or of contact for short time periods, is less.[27] In pig farming, behavioral problems commonly arise when boars are grouped together. In contrast, in the wild, boars live in isolation from other boars, except during the breeding season, which, in Europe, peaks in December.[28] Their relations with other boars are therefore minimal. When farmed, boars live relatively peaceably if socialized as piglets and kept together in the same group. In a Swedish study, the boars that were reared in this way were observed to display aggressive behavior far less frequently than those

23. Berardinelli and Tauck, "Intensity," 30–31.
24. Animal Welfare Committee, Opinion, 167–72, 35–36.
25. Kenyon et al., "Effect."
26. Brooks and Cole, "The Effect."
27. Hughes et al., "Mechanisms."
28. Dardaillon, "Wild Boar Social Groupings."

that had been mixed at later ages. Moreover, as few as 13 percent suffered skins lesions as a result of aggressive interactions, compared with 74 percent of the control group. Where such lesions occurred, these were typically much less severe than in the control group. These striking findings suggest that there is no intrinsic need to castrate farmed boars.

Another reason that is given for boar castration is meat flavor. However, because flavor is influenced by feed type, the wish to improve it is not sufficient grounds for castration. "Boar taint" may be reduced by altering the feeding regime prior to slaughter, thus removing the need for castration in infancy. The most significant chemicals that determine flavor are skatole, which is a by-product of microbial breakdown in the large intestine, and the testicular steroid androstenone. Both enter blood plasma and accumulate in fatty tissue, leading to an odor when meat from the slaughtered animal is cooked that is often considered unpleasant. Providing organically fed pigs with 25 percent of their daily energy intake as crude or dried chopped chicory roots, which are high in the prebiotic inulin, for even just one week before slaughter, has been found to eliminate skatole almost completely.[29] Furthermore, in the same suite of experiments, boars that were fed crude chicory for nine weeks before slaughter exhibited androstenone levels that were much lower than in the control group. In a different experimental series, feeding boars 30 percent raw potato starch during the week before slaughter resulted in 74 percent skatole reduction.[30] These findings indicate that good meat flavor does not require castration.

Among all farmed species, the physical separation of adults by sex prevents mating while avoiding the need for castrating males, or even vasectomizing them.[31] It is certainly a less expensive option than vasectomy, which is economically unfeasible at scale. Gaps in fencing that are high enough for young to pass under, but are too low for adult animals, may allow young to move freely

29. Hansen et al., "Influence."
30. Pauly et al., "Performances."
31. Kiley, "A Review," 325.

between the male and female adult groups, supporting both milk feeding and group socialization.

2. Tails

In ancient Israel, as today, female farm animals were not generally castrated. Performing this operation on females is much more difficult and does not bring the perceived management or behavioral benefits that are associated with castrating males. Moreover, castration would have prevented female ruminants from giving birth, and therefore from producing milk, both of which would have greatly reduced their production value. The fact that the Bible specifies in several instances (enumerated in chapter 2.1) that female animals must be unmutilated, therefore, indicates other concerns. For either a male or a female animal to be *tamim*, it must not have undergone a mutilation of any kind. In ancient Israel, by far the most widespread mutilation performed on female farm animals was the tail-docking of sheep.

The only native sheep breed was the Awassi, which still predominates in Israel, Palestine, and the surrounding region. It is identifiable by its large fat tail (*alyah*), which serves, similarly to a camel's hump, as a storage reserve during periods of food scarcity.[32] The tail thus helps sheep to survive and, in the case of ewes, to feed their young. Because fat is stored within it, less fat accumulates elsewhere on the body, which aids cooling. A large tail may also shelter the head of a flockmate when a group is resting close together in sunny and hot conditions.[33] However, a large tail also hinders flight from predators. This suggests that such a tail is a product of domestication in steppe locations that were seasonally challenging but where shepherds protected flocks from predators. Within the ancient Israelite sacrificial system, it was regarded as essential that sheep retained their entire tail through their whole

32. Epstein, *The Awassi Sheep*, 1–6; Borowski, *Every Living Thing*, 66–67.
33. Epstein, *The Awassi Sheep*, 46.

lifetime until slaughter. The ordination, wellbeing, and guilt offerings of a ram each included its fat tail.[34]

In farm animals, tails serve several purposes, which vary between species. These include aiding posture, rectal function, and locomotion. Among pigs and cattle, postural change is usually a combined motion of the head and tail.[35] Use of the tail to aid locomotion was important among the wild ancestors of these farmed species, which would have needed to be able to escape predators at speed and to negotiate varied terrains during seasonal migration and while searching for food.

Another practical use of the tail is the protection of other body parts. Among pigs and cattle, tail movement is a response to skin irritation.[36] By brushing its tail against its body, a pig or bovine may attempt to remove the cause of the irritation, which might be flies, flora, or soil. Success is likely to increase physical comfort and to reduce disease risk. Cattle probably find their tails more useful for this purpose than pigs. This is because theirs are longer and are therefore able to brush against a greater proportion of the body. Adult sheep have thicker tails than pigs or cattle. These shield their anus and external reproductive organs from wet, cold, and direct sunlight, and, in the case of ewes, protect their udders.[37] Tails are also deployed in display and ritual. Among goats, tail wagging by does arouses bucks, stimulating their interest and interaction.[38] Pigs and cattle elevate their tails during courtship.[39]

Tail raising or wagging is also an important indicator of contentment among both adults and young. Pigs and cattle may elevate their tails in response to the tactile stimulation of their back by a herdmate or a human, and sows frequently raise their tails during suckling. Most lambs wag their tails, especially when nosing, and

---

34. Exod 29:22; Lev 3:9; 7:3; 8:25; 9:19.

35. Kiley-Worthington, "Tail Movements," 73–76.

36. Kiley-Worthington, "Tail Movements," 88.

37. Scholtz and Cloete, "The Lamb's Tail."

38. Haulenbeek and Katz, "Female Tail Wagging."

39. Kiley-Worthington, "Tail Movements," 77–78.

while suckling or otherwise in the company of the dam.[40] Free-ranging piglets in Scotland were observed to spend increasing amounts of time during their first fourteen weeks of life wagging their tails, with females doing so for twice as long as boars.[41] Domestically bred pigs are able to curl their tail, but pigs in the wild do not, suggesting that this characteristic is due to domestication. Research with the Casertana breed of pigs, which is concentrated in southern Italy, in which some animals have curled tails but others have straight tails, suggests that tail curling is due to selection for genetically associated characteristics.[42] In experiments, tail curling has been linked with good quality accommodation, generous provision of rooting substratum, thermal comfort, object play, social play, and positive contact with a familiar stockperson.[43]

In this section, and in chapter 2.1, it has been seen that leaving male animals entire, and allowing the tails of both males and females to remain intact, feature prominently in Old Testament accounts of how farm animals that were offered to God as a sacrifice, whether in the Jerusalem temple or by households, were to be presented. It would be unrealistic to suppose that all farm animals experienced such high welfare. Had these practices been universal, it would have been unnecessary to reiterate their importance as frequently as the Bible does. Nevertheless, given the number of animals that were offered each year at the temple and by households, these requirements significantly influenced husbandry practices. Once an animal had been either castrated or tail docked, there was no possibility that it could be sacrificially offered, and therefore an important potential source of revenue for its owner was removed. The husbandry requirements for sacrificial animals are thus likely to have had significant positive effects on the welfare of all farm animals.

40. Vince, "Response."
41. Newberry and Wood-Gush, "Development," 106.
42. Bertolini et al., "Exploiting Phenotype Diversity."
43. Camerlink and Ursinus, "Tail Postures," 2, 4.

3. Horns

The *tamim* principle extends beyond issues related to castration and tail-docking, calling into question any mutilation that deprives an animal of the use of parts of its body. It suggests the strong desirability, on welfare grounds, of preserving intact other parts of farm animal bodies. Basil of Caesarea, whose awareness of the skills and sensory perception of farm animals was noted in chapters 1.1 and 1.2, writes: "The calf has not yet horns, but he knows where nature has implanted his instruments."[44] This fourth-century bishop and theologian recognizes that horn growth is a natural part of cattle development, and that horns serve purposes. In cattle, they are of great importance in establishing social hierarchy. Among twenty-five changing groups of four dairy heifers, based on interactions indicating dominance and submission, as well as on feeding competition, horns were found to be an even more significant indicator of position than body weight, with light animals bearing horns occupying a significantly higher average social rank than heavy animals with no horns.[45] Cattle also use their horns for self-grooming, and even to open food sources on farms.[46]

Among sheep and goats, horns signify social rank as well as being deployed in confrontations for both defensive shielding and as offensive weapons.[47] Via combats, male access to females, and thus the ability to reproduce, are controlled. Horn structure is closely related to skull morphology, with the horn and skull together absorbing high impact blows. In the biblical world, combats were viewed as a sufficiently characteristic behavior of rams, or *karim*, that the same term is used to designate the battering rams with which an army would breach city gates or walls in battle.[48]

---

44. Basil, "On the Hexameron" 9.4, 142. With reference to Rom 6:13, I translate *hopla* as instruments rather than as weapons.

45. Bouissou, "Influence."

46. Knierim et al., "To Be," 31.

47. Shackleton and Shank, "A Review."

48. Ezek 4:2; 21:22.

However, the principal purpose of sheep horns appears, like cattle horns, to be to maintain a stable and peaceable social structure.[49] Among free-ranging mountain sheep observed in Canada over four seasons, horn display was mostly directed by larger-horned rams toward smaller-horned rams. Moreover, sheep socialized with those with similar-sized horns.

Among all farmed ruminant species, horns also fulfill a thermoregulatory function. Because a large surface area of the horn relative to volume is in contact with the air, when warm blood is pumped around the horn core, the blood temperature falls.[50] By means of this mechanism, an animal is able to transmit heat away from its body to the air, and thus to cool itself. This helps to explain why, in global perspective, wild sheep species inhabiting cold environments generally have smaller horn cores relative to body mass than those living in hot climates.[51] Moreover, among a group of Pyrenean Brown beef calves, an inverse correlation was found between horn size and ear size. This suggests that animals with either small horns or no horns may grow larger ears, which also aid cooling, in order to compensate.[52] This is because, in ears, the development of new blood vessels out of existing ones enables blood to circulate close to the outside of the body.

4. Piglet Teeth and Pig Snouts

In the Old Testament, pigs are presented as unclean, which suggests that they were not domesticated. Archeological evidence indicates that pigs were indeed not much farmed in the southern kingdom of Judah, which was centred on Jerusalem, where the Jewish religious authorities, including the scholars and scribes who composed the Bible, were located. In contrast, there is some

---

49. Geist, "The Evolutionary Significance."
50. Taylor, "The Vascularity."
51. Hoefs, "The Thermoregulatory Potential."
52. Parés-Casanova and Caballero, "Possible Tendency."

evidence of pig farming in the northern kingdom of Israel.[53] It is within, or near, the territory that historically constituted this kingdom that Jesus is described as sending demons into a herd of pigs, which then run down a slope into a lake, where they drown.[54] Even so, the body morphology of pigs receives no detailed biblical discussion. Nevertheless, in the post-biblical era, even Christian communities that took Old Testament law very seriously permitted the farming, slaughter, and human consumption of pigs, especially in regions such as Ireland, where pork was a staple food.[55] It is therefore reasonable to apply the biblical *tamim* principle in the Christian context to mutilations that are particular to pigs. Indeed, piglets frequently undergo more mutilations that any other farm animal, typically experiencing, within their first week of life, teeth clipping, tail docking, and, if they are male, castration. At an older age, those living outdoors may also have their nose pierced so that a ring may be attached to it. Castration and tail docking were discussed in chapters 2.1 and 2.2, but these additional interventions now require comment.

Piglets are born with eight sharp "needle" teeth comprising four canines and four incisors. These enable them to compete to suckle from a teat, preferably one closest to the front of the sow, from which the greatest volume of milk may be obtained. As piglets grow toward maturity, these are replaced by permanent teeth. Although the birth teeth are often removed soon after birth, they perform important functions. Being born with teeth may increase the survival chances of the smaller piglets within a litter, especially in a first litter, or where the sow is older.[56] Teeth enable self-defense against aggression by larger littermates and have the effect of facilitating teat access by smaller piglets. They do not appear to increase the number of lesions on the bodies of littermates, although cause some lesion damage to sow teats.[57] The latter is most likely to occur

---

53. Sapir-Hen et al., "Pig Husbandry."
54. Matt 8:30–32; Mark 5:11–13; Luke 8:32–33.
55. Grumett, "Mosaic Food Rules."
56. Bates et al., "The Influence."
57. Fu et al., "Effects."

in litters where, due to inadequate feeding, the sow's milk supply is insufficient for the number of piglets, or where the number of teats is fewer than the number of piglets. This suggests that, rather than removing teeth, breeding genetics that increase litter size to a level at which the number of piglets born cannot be easily nursed by their sow should be avoided and, where necessary, reversed.

For much of their waking day, pigs living in natural settings engage in purposeful activity. In Scotland, over a three-year period spent studying thirteen groups in a varied environment that included forest, gorse, bog, and open grass, individual animals were grazing at 31 percent of observations, rooting at 21 percent, and nosing or orienting to stimuli at 8 percent.[58] All these activities require use of the snout, even though this is sometimes ringed in order to inhibit activity that might be deemed to damage the surrounding environment, by making this painful.[59] Grazing, rooting, and nosing involve sniffing the ground, touching its surface, or items on it, with the flat end of the snout, and digging into the ground with the snout's front edge.[60] They are basic to feeding but also form part of normal behavioral repertoire, being means by which pigs interact with their surroundings and maintain their physical movement. In the same study, piglets were observed to sniff and forage from two weeks of age, trotting and scampering while doing so.[61] In a Spanish evergreen oak forest during the course of two autumns and winters, pigs without feed supplement mainly grazed on grass and foraged acorns, taking numerous small bites, with foraging occupying an average of 60 percent of their time.[62] The total time taken is similar to that in the Scottish location just described, where alternative available items, such as

---

58. Stolba and Wood-Gush, "The Behaviour."

59. Snout ringing is presented in Prov 11:22 (NIV) for the purpose of pejorative comparison: "Like a gold ring in a pig's snout is a beautiful woman who shows no discretion."

60. Horrell et al., "The Use."

61. Newberry and Wood-Gush, "Development."

62. Rodríguez-Estévez et al., "Foraging."

small roots, were also sought.[63] In addition, if needed within a specific environment, pigs use their snouts to dig out wallows, which is essentially large-scale rooting. Cumulatively, these normal behaviors are likely to bring about considerable soil disturbance and displacement across the area in which pigs are accommodated. Nevertheless, the fact that pigs use their snouts for such a wide range of normal activities suggests that they should not be ringed, but that animals should be stocked and managed so as to ensure that the area in which they live does not sustain excessive damage.

5. Chicken Beaks

The beaks of domestic chickens comprise upper and lower parts. The upper part is fused to the skull and curves and closes over the lower mandible, which is hinged and so may move up and down, and both parts have sharp pointed tips. Chicken beaks are often trimmed, in order to reduce the aggressive pecking of flockmates housed in close conditions. However, the beak morphology just described allows chickens and other birds to grasp and relocate small items of flora, such as the leaf that the dove picks and brings to Noah following the Flood, as a sign that vegetation is re-growing.[64] It allows birds to feed efficiently, such as when lifting grains or feed pellets from the ground.[65] The first stage of this movement is pecking, when the bird lunges, opening its beak around the pellet and pushing down into the substratum, so that the beak surrounds the pellet. The pellet is then grasped, with the beak beginning to close while lifting upward. Following this rapid motion is a longer period in the closed beak, during which beak and tongue movements direct the pellet toward the back of the mouth before swallowing. Beak activity is a major part of chicken behavior. As already indicated, its primary purpose is feeding. In semi-wild zoo conditions that included trees, bushes, and clearings, chickens observed over

63. Stolba and Wood-Gush, "The Behaviour."
64. Gen 8:11.
65. Gentle et al., "The Effect."

two years spent 60 percent of their active time ground-pecking.[66] Chickens also use their beaks for self-grooming, which aligns the barbs that grow off the main shaft of each feather in order to improve their effectiveness for regulating body temperature and waterproofing. By touching their preen gland with their beak before doing so, chickens are able, at the same time, to apply the waxy oil that it produces to their feathers. Preening reduces the incidence of disease by guarding against external parasitic infection and spread on individual birds, through the flock, and potentially to humans.[67]

Farmers and researchers have identified several ways to promote the peaceful coexistence of chickens.[68] Within housing, light levels should be dim, with good building maintenance and the repair of electrical lighting eliminating localized areas of bright light. Diet is also important. Changes to it should be avoided, and a sufficient number of feeding points should be provided to eliminate competition for feed. Feed should be offered in mash form, which encourages foraging behavior, and should possess a high fibre content. The indoor temperature should be kept uniformly warm so that birds do not have to compete for comfortable space. Well-designed accommodation and well-managed feeding are likely to eliminate the need for beak trimming.

6. Breeding Bodies

So far in this chapter, it has been shown how the bodies of individual animals may be altered by several forms of mutilation. They may also be changed at the group level by selective breeding. Farm animals were selectively bred in biblical times. On parting from his father-in-law Laban, Jacob understandably wishes to establish his own flock. He petitions Laban to permit him to remove only

66. Wiltschko et al., "The Magnetic Compass."
67. Chen et al., "Beak Condition."
68. Kaukonen and Valros, "Feather Pecking."

45

the speckled and spotted sheep and goats, and the black lambs.[69] Laban accepts, because, it may be inferred, these animals probably then formed, as is normal for the region, as little as 10 percent of the flock.[70] However, Laban then removes all these animals from the flock so that Jacob cannot take them. But Jacob does not give up establishing his own herd. He was a hardworking stockperson who had gained much experience during years spent working for his father-in-law. Moreover, as a twin[71] he may have reflected on possible mechanisms of heredity, identity, and difference. Jacob establishes his own breeding programme, constructing wooden fences to segregate animals and, by mating ewes with black and speckled rams, selects for speckled and spotted animals, which, being crossbred, are stronger.[72] The speckled (*naqod*) flock of Jacob becomes larger and more productive than the white (*laban*) flock of his father-in-law, who, it may be assumed, had no breeding strategy.[73] Jacob subsequently delivers to his twin brother Esau a peace offering that includes some of these animals in a proportion of ten ewes to one ram.[74] This provides further evidence that Jacob understands the principles of selective breeding, and especially the importance of keeping high quality males.

Jacob's breeding programme promotes herd health, and therefore benefits both the flock and its future members. Moreover, as a result of his gift to Esau, at least one other flock comes into being, with its own structure and social life. This in turn also becomes large.[75] However, another Old Testament example of a

69. Gen 30:32—31:12; Borowski, *Every Living Thing*, 50–51.

70. Levin, "Albinism." In any case, if the subset of animals had been any more than a small minority of the total herd, Laban would have rejected his son-in-law's proposal.

71. Gen 25:21–26.

72. Pearson, "A Mendelian Interpretation." A few interpreters have argued that the water in which the wooden stems are steeped, which the animals drink from the trough while breeding, directly influences the breeding outcome. Although the text allows this explanation, it seems implausible.

73. For the word play, Park, "Transformation."

74. Gen 32:13–14.

75. Gen 36:7.

selectively bred characteristic has negative welfare implications. In chapter 2.2, I discussed the large fat tail (*alyah*) of Awassi sheep, which hinders flight from predators. The biblical strictures against removing these tails from sacrificial animals while they were alive indicate that they were considered an edible delicacy. For instance, the tail is included in the portion that the prophet Samuel reserves for Saul at the feast that is thrown the night before his anointing as king.[76] As a result of breeding for human consumption, the size and weight of these tails became so great that the flourishing of the animals bearing them was undermined. Classical sources, which may be exaggerated, suggest that tails could reach one hundred and thirty centimeters in length and weigh ninety pounds.[77] Shepherds constructed wooden trolleys, which looked like small carts, to attach to sheep via a harness, which aided locomotion by keeping the tail clear of the ground. Prohibiting the removal of fat tails prior to sacrifice suggests that these body parts were recognized to be intrinsic to the sheep.

These contrasting biblical examples indicate that breeding strategies may be either good or bad for the welfare of individual farm animals and for animal groups. An example of a selective breeding outcome with a negative impact on welfare is increased sow litter size, which was discussed in chapter 2.4. Another is breeding meat chickens with bodies that are too large and heavy to be supported by their legs. Breeding strategies should be pursued that protect farm animal welfare and do not pursue production outcomes and business performance at the cost of welfare.

7. Lifespan

In the Old Testament, animals that have attained full maturity frequently appear and are acceptable for sacrifice. A three-year-old heifer, goat, and ram are each offered by Abraham after he is told

76. 1 Sam 9:24. See Gootwine, *Physical Appearance*. This volume includes photographs of mosaics, statues, and carvings.

77. Goodridge, "The Case." This article includes illustrations.

that he will have issue and thus an heir.[78] Abraham later appropriates a ram caught by its horns in the thicket to offer in place of his son Isaac, and a ram forms part of the monthly Israelite sacrifice.[79] Indeed, rams (*ayilim*) appear in the Old Testament as many as 183 times. Jacob's reminder to his father-in-law Laban that he has not eaten his rams indicates that they were regarded as a desirable source of food and breeding genetics that should be preserved.[80]

The species for which there is the greatest contrast between slaughter age in the biblical period and today is sheep. The slaughter of lambs for human consumption was rare and is explicitly censured by the prophet Amos.[81] Lambs were highly prized because they would grow into sheep that would produce milk, fleece, and potentially a larger quantity of meat. For this reason, they are among the valuable items that Saul and his army take after defeating the Amalekites, and are elsewhere described as being traded with princes and sent to rulers.[82] The fat of lambs is part of the imagery of divine abundance that Moses describes as being shown to Jacob.[83] Until recently, sheep were frequently not slaughtered until several years of age, and, into the 1950s, mutton rather than lamb was the generic designation for sheep meat in England.[84] Moreover, English cookbooks show that mutton was far more commonly used than lamb, with slaughter typically occurring at four years. At this classic age, ewes would have bred perhaps three times and their meat, especially in the case of mountain breeds, would have been lean and flavorsome. A traditional method of cooking well-hung, four-year-old mutton was to rub the joint with black pepper, thyme, mace, and meal, wrap it, roast slowly, and remove the wrapping for browning and crisping.[85] At this age,

78. Gen 15:9; see Borowski, *Every Living Thing*, 220–21.
79. Gen 22:13; Num 28:11.
80. Gen 31:38.
81. Amos 6:4.
82. 1 Sam 15:9; Ezek 27:21; Isa 16:1.
83. Deut 32:14.
84. Hartley, *Food*, 135–63.
85. Hartley, *Food*, 142–43.

mutton was known as "eight-tooth," because the animal providing it would have acquired all four pairs of its lower incisors, but these would not have begun to spread and fall out. However, nowadays sheep are usually slaughtered at less than a year of age, and their meat is therefore described as lamb.

There is a wide lack of understanding of what a normal lifespan for each farm animal species might be, or how this might be determined, given that it is an outcome of the interaction of several factors including nutrition, body size, medication use, and genetics.[86] Nevertheless, for farmed species, comparison with wild relatives provides a reasonable indication. In the wild, animals typically live much longer than on farms, because they are not slaughtered once a specified bodyweight is reached or their secondary production has fallen below a required level. Wild conditions provide a more justifiable comparison than an optimized domesticated situation until death from natural causes, in which an animal would effectively be kept as a pet rather than to provide its keeper with food or income. Among a wild boar population studied near Warsaw, the greatest recorded lifespan was nine years.[87] However, most animals died much younger due to factors including low temperatures, seasonal food shortages, parasitic infections, and males fighting each other. The shortest-lived farm animal is the chicken, which is frequently slaughtered at five weeks of age. In a free-ranging population at San Diego Zoo, the average lifespan of hens that reared chicks to independence was, in contrast, approximately three years.[88] Chickens that are not slaughtered for meat usually die of respiratory diseases. Among brown trout sampled in Norwegian rivers, average longevity was between 4.7 years and 11.1 years.[89] In more northerly latitudes, trout tend to live longer, probably because the colder water temperatures slow their metabolism and growth to maturity. Cattle are by far the longest lived and longest breeding farm animal. Dental analysis suggests that

86. Hoffman and Valencak, "A Short Life."
87. Jezierski, "Longevity."
88. Collias et al., "Dominant Red Junglefowl."
89. Jonsson et al., "Longevity."

individuals of some breeds may live up to thirty-six years, with native British breeds frequently living, and often calving, into their late teens.[90]

These lifespans, which are much longer than those to be found on farms, raise significant ethical and welfare questions. Animals, birds, and fish that are slaughtered young in order to maximize financial returns are not able to have as many positive life experiences as those that are allowed to live for longer. It is also likely that, in very young animal herds and flocks, group structure and learning are less well developed, impeding group functioning.

8. Conclusion

Depending on their species, farm animals may be either born with, or grow, tails, horns, snouts, teeth, beaks, and reproductive organs. In the introduction to this chapter, many functions were listed that these body parts allow animals to perform. These included rooting, pecking, removing sources of irritation or potential disease, heating and cooling, protecting other body parts, displaying social status, defense and attack, and reproduction. In this chapter, how the different farm animal species use body parts to perform these functions has been described. The duration between birth and death, during which animals that are farmed may in principle exercise these functions, has also been discussed.

In one or more farmed species, each one of these functions is either frequently undermined, or made impossible, by different kinds of mutilation. These may often be well-intended and informed by traditional understandings of herd or flock management and risk reduction. Mutilations are performed in order to reduce the risks or hazards that are related to breeding, disease, animal behavior, human health and safety, and habitat. However, they are likely to inhibit animal flourishing and even to make basic living difficult, with any behavioral, biosecurity, or management advantages that are gained by a particular mutilation being

---

90. Jones and Sadler, "A Review," 7–8.

offset by welfare problems and limitations on the ability to express normal behavior. All types of mutilation of farm animals should be greatly reduced from their current levels, limited to essential, exceptional occasions, and undertaken only with appropriate measures to avoid animals experiencing pain at the time of the procedure or at any future point in their life as a consequence of it.

3

Behavior

BEHAVIORAL NORMS ARE EMBEDDED in most aspects of a farm animal's life. In chapter 1, it was shown that a distinguishing mark of domesticated species is their group identity, with young being socialized into the group. The group also provides the setting for courtship and mating. Around the time when young are born, some species display distinctive nesting behaviors, and all demonstrate maternal care. In chapter 2, it was shown that bodies and behavioral repertoire are inextricably linked, with examples including movement, grooming, rooting, pecking, and sexual expression. The purpose of this chapter is to address aspects of behavior that are not directly associated with group identity, reproduction, or individual bodily parts.

A notable feature of farm animal species is that almost all are precocial, that is, they exhibit a degree of independence from birth and develop characteristic behaviors from an extremely young age. No commonly farmed species is altricial, that is, underdeveloped at birth and dependent on parental support for rapid postnatal development. Wild animals may, in contrast, be either precocial or, like rodents and carnivores, altricial. Precocity in simple behaviors is strong evidence that behavior is innate to farmed species. Among ruminants, rising and standing so that the dam's udder and teats may be reached is an obvious example. Most lambs stand upright within thirty minutes of birth.[1] In a study of Swedish Holstein calves, the median duration from birth to standing was fifty-three minutes.[2] During observation of a group of newborn goats at a research institute near Cambridge, the time from birth to first standing ranged from nineteen to 203 minutes.[3] These are vastly quicker timings than for humans, not just as simple duration but as a proportion of lifespan. Also notable is the young age from which chicks are likely to begin to scratch, perch, run, and socialize independently of the hen, and to move out of her sight. A field study suggests that this rapid development occurs as early as ten days of age.[4]

This chapter will examine the behavioral aspects of habitat, feeding, migration, and route-finding. Each could be instrumentally regarded as arbitrarily chosen with the aim of meeting survival needs. However, the habitat and feed that are suited to different farm animal species and the journeys that animals undertake are functions of their biological and physiological needs. The chapter will end with a discussion of play. This is superfluous to basic functioning but, for precisely this reason, forms part of a life worth living for farm animals.

1. Habitat

In the Genesis 1 creation narrative, the first four days are occupied by the lighting, watering, and planting of the earth, and the inaugurating of days and seasons, to establish habitats, on which the living creatures (*nephesh chayyah*), which are created on the fifth and sixth days, depend for life and growth. In the narrative, the primary function of the earth is to support sentient life. On the third day, the seas are made, and, on the fifth day, they are

---

1. Vince, "Response," 165–66.
2. Ventorp and Michanek, "Cow-Calf Behaviour."
3. Stephens and Linzell, "The Development."
4. Workman and Andrew, "Simultaneous Changes."

populated with living creatures.⁵ On the same day, dry land appears, and plants and trees grow on it. The plants and trees, it may be presumed, provide shelter, shade, nesting materials, and landmarks for the birds that are brought forth on the fifth day, and for the land animals that are made on the sixth day. In the Genesis 2 creation narrative, a river is depicted flowing out of Eden and dividing into four, suggesting a freshwater habitat in addition to the seas of the preceding chapter.⁶

When God blesses Noah and his offspring following the Flood, living creatures are explicitly identified with different habitats: the animals of the land (*chayyah ha'arets*), the birds of the air (*oph hashamayim*), and the fish of the sea (*dag hayyam*).⁷ The food rules outlined in Leviticus 11:2b–19 and Deuteronomy 14:3–20 each depend on classification by habitat. This is most obviously signalled in the order of exposition, which moves from land animals, to birds, and then to fish, and follows the order in which the animals are entrusted to Noah. A small qualification is that, in Leviticus, it is recognized that fish may inhabit streams (*nechalim*) as well as seas.⁸ It is notable that the animals are assigned habitats that are all outdoors, and that at no future point is any other norm established. This does not mean that animals must not be kept indoors. On the contrary, in ancient Israel, human dwellings frequently included space that was periodically occupied by animals. The biblical norm of outdoor rearing does, however, suggest that indoor housing is likely to require justification on the grounds that it improves animal welfare in particular situations of limited duration, such as adverse weather conditions. Also relevant to habitat is the requirement that, in order to be considered clean, a land animal must possess a cloven or divided hoof.⁹ This horny part of

---

5. Gen 1:9–13.

6. Gen 2:10–14.

7. Gen 9:2–3; also Ps 8:7–8; Ezek 38:20; Matt 6:26.

8. Lev 11:9.

9. Lev 11:3; Deut 14:6. See Douglas, "The Forbidden Animals," 16; Douglas, *Purity and Danger*, 56.

the foot of a ruminant animal makes it well-suited to grazing on pasture or to browsing plants, including on moist but firm ground. An outdoor habitat potentially allows animals that range across wide areas to do so freely. This is especially important for pigs and turkeys. When selecting a nesting location, a sow or gilt may travel several kilometers to explore possible sites. A nesting location should, like any area where pigs may settle, provide water to support wallowing, which is recognized in the second letter of Peter as a normal pig behavior.[10] During one observation, approximately twenty-four hours before farrowing, females that had been fitted with radio transmitters undertook investigations lasting four to six hours, during which they traveled 2.5–6.5 kilometers over a large but bounded range.[11] About a day prior to that, they perambulated at the edge of the normal activity area and away from the group at a distance of several hundred meters. In a study conducted in an Arkansas wildlife park during the February to July breeding and rearing season, female wild turkeys inhabiting a mixed evergreen and deciduous highland forest that included clearings, pasture, and some fields, were captured using nets, fitted with radio transmitters, and then released. They were estimated to have traversed an average area of nineteen square kilometers.[12] Young adults moved over an even greater area of, on average, thirty-two square kilometers. Nesting females traveled an average of four hundred meters each day, while those not nesting moved only around two hundred and fifty meters. This is because they were engaged in nesting-site selection and nest-building activities similar to those of the sows previously described, seeking locations that were safe from predators and that provided good-quality forage. The distance between the nesting sites that were selected from one year to the next was even greater, being on average 2.4 kilometers for mature females but almost nine kilometers for those that were younger. The heavier females, which were also dominant and

10. 2 Pet 2:22.
11. Jensen, "Observations."
12. Thogmartin, "Home-Range Size."

older, undertook the shortest nesting journeys, because they were better able to secure desirable sites close to the main group.

For chickens, the ground surface substrate is extremely important for maintaining plumage condition. Dustbathing is a key behavioral need that is performed about once every two days and lasts approximately twenty minutes.[13] It removes stale feather lipids, which are the oils that condition and waterproof the feathers. Preferred substrates, such as sand and peat, are composed of small particles. Dustbathing frequency rapidly increases during the second week of life, when it is performed two to three times per day, but decreases back to its normal level by the fourth week. The bird scratches the substrate and rakes it with its beak. It progressively erects its feathers and squats, then vertically shakes its wings, rubs its head, beak-rakes again, and scratches with one leg. When finished, the bird arises and shakes off the dust. Maintaining good plumage condition is important for cooling and warming, and for flight. In the wild, appropriate substrates will be more readily available in some environments. In a national park in India, birds of the same species displayed a marked preference for mixed forest and forested grassland habitats.[14]

For goats, the browsing of plants and trees is an important part of normal behavior. Whereas sheep graze and forage mostly within fifty centimeters of ground level, even during winter, when the food supply may be limited, goats frequently rise up on their hind legs to seek food at one meter and may reach as high as 1.5 meters.[15] Furthermore, whereas sheep consume grass and herbaceous plants, goats forage extensively among woody plants all year round, including when pasture is readily available. They may perform the useful ecological function of limiting the growth of woody saplings and undergrowth. However, if land is stocked too densely, and goats are not moved with sufficient frequency, they are likely to consume vegetation more quickly than it regrows. The complementary feeding behaviors of sheep and goats help

13. Olsson and Keeling, "Why in Earth?"
14. Javed and Rahmani, "Flocking."
15. Plessis et al., "A Comparison."

to explain why, as was discussed in chapter 1.1, these two species have often been accommodated together, including in biblical accounts, and have been referred to generically.

Overall, the Bible gives considerable attention to animal habitat and recognizes that different farm animal species have characteristic habitats. Both the substrate that a particular habitat provides, and, for some species, the size of the area that is available for ranging, are important requirements for enabling normal behavior.

2. Feeding

On the third day of the Genesis 1 creation narrative, God commands the earth to grow (*dasha*) vegetation (*deshe*). This includes plants (*eseb*) yielding seed (*zera*) and trees producing fruit (*peri*), which are all seen by God to be good.[16] On the sixth day, the land animals and birds are given all the green plants (*yereq eseb*) for food.[17] Thus is established a close linkage between habitat and food: the food that animals are to eat is naturally available in their habitat. Grazed and browsed vegetation is thus presented as the normal foodstuff for farm animals and birds. Nevertheless, the fattening of individual cattle kept indoors is elsewhere referred to several times. The term for fatted is *marbeq*, and literally refers to a stall or tying place. When the starving king Saul visits a seer in order to learn his fate in the impeding battle with the Philistines, she kills a fatted calf, which she has housed within her dwelling, for him and his servants.[18] In a reference that is apparently to the high quality of their body condition, and to their wish to escape their predicament, the paid soldiers of Egypt are compared with stall cattle.[19] Eating stall-finished calves is explicitly censured by the prophet

16. Gen 1:11–12. For further discussion, see Grumett, "Food."

17. Gen 1:30.

18. 1 Sam 28:24.

19. Jer 46:21. The context is the advance of the Babylonian army against Egypt.

Amos, who associates the practice with excessive luxury.[20] He thus presents a direct link between extravagant human consumption and the confinement of animals in unnatural accommodation, for the purpose of reducing their opportunities for exercise while feeding them concentrated ration to promote weight gain. In order to preserve their rumen health and to prevent the accumulation of acid in the stomach, the amount of grain concentrate consumed by cattle must be carefully managed as part of a balanced diet.[21] Although chickens have, like humans, a stomach with a single chamber rather than several, fibre is also important for their digestion. The structure it adds to ingested food aids the development of the gizzard—which is an organ within the digestive canal that grinds food, and which is necessary because birds do not have teeth—and promotes the functioning of digestive enzymes. Fibre also improves gut microflora and health, and nutrient utilization.[22] Pigs benefit from a mixed diet including sufficient bulky and fermentable fibre, which is also important for them for behavioral reasons. Unlike a diet that is highly reliant on grain concentrates, a mixed diet induces satiety, and thereby reduces physical activity after eating and other stereotypical behaviors, such as chewing, which are likely to contribute to conflicts within a group.[23]

In the Old Testament, whether a particular species may be farmed and consumed by humans depends on its diet. In order to be regarded as clean, one of the criteria that animals must satisfy is that they chew the cud. The additional requirement, that an animal must possess a divided, or cloven, hoof, which has already been discussed in chapter 3.1 in relation to habitat, serves to emphasize this criterion.[24] For a land animal, the most likely alternative to a cloven hoof is a claw, which is a feature of predatory animals that enables them to catch prey and to climb above ground level in

20. Mal 4:2; Amos 6:4; also Hab 3:17, which uses *repheth*. Borowski, *Every Living Thing*, 58, 77–78.

21. Hernández et al., "Ruminal Acidosis."

22. Kheravii et al., "Roles."

23. Leeuw et al., "Effects."

24. Douglas, "The Forbidden Animals," 17–18.

order to observe potential quarry. The absence of a claw suggests that an animal is of a ruminant, non-predatory species.

The renowned Alexandrian biblical exegete Origen exhibits a sophisticated understanding of rumination, using this to represent how the Bible is to be reflected on. Citing Psalm 1:2, he states that "one is said to chew the cud who pays heed to knowledge and 'meditates day and night on the Law of the Lord.'" Origen continues that a human who, as it were, chews the cud, "applies those things which he reads according to the letter to the spiritual sense and . . . ascends from the lowest and visible to the invisible and higher things."[25] An accomplished Hebraist, Origen would certainly have understood that the term for chewing the cud, *ma'alat gerah*, does not primarily describe the biting and breaking down of food in the mouth. Rather, it literally refers to the "bringing up" of the cud, employing a root *alah* that appears in several different contexts and is frequently used to signify rising or ascent.[26] This digestive process is made possible because cattle, sheep, and goats each have four chambers within their stomach, including the rumen and the reticulum. During rumination, after fibrous food first enters the rumen, it is broken down and passes into the reticulum, where it is mixed with saliva and brought back up into the mouth for further chewing. It is this digestive understanding of ascent that Origen uses to image the time-consuming spiritual ascent of the mind from earthly reality to heavenly things.

As was suggested in chapter 3.1 in the discussion of the substrate that a habitat provides, it would be wrong to regard feeding as nothing more than the satisfaction of a need to ingest nutrition. Grazing or, out of season, consuming conserved pasture, occupies a major portion of a ruminant animal's daily activity and is an important general and oral behavior. It is referred to in the Bible on many occasions.[27] The recognition that food ingestion is a natural

25. Origen, *Homilies on Leviticus, 1–16*, 7.6 (2), 148. The Hebrew verb *hagah* suggests a form of meditation that includes moving and speaking with the mouth, and which is therefore not restricted to inward mental activity.

26. Lev 11:3–6; Deut 14:6.

27. E.g., Gen 37:13, 16; Num 35:2–7; Josh 14:4; 21:1–42; 1 Chr 4:39–40;

behavior may lie behind the injunction not to muzzle an ox while it is treading out the grain from the husks.[28] Among steers observed in Japan and New South Wales, eating accounted for at least 95 percent of oral behaviors on all five farms studied where the animals grazed pasture, regardless of its quality. However, among a penned group that was offered both grain concentrate and hay in separate troughs, this proportion dropped to 77 percent, with a far greater incidence of behaviors including self-grooming, social grooming, licking objects, and tongue playing, in order to compensate activity loss.[29] These behaviors were concentrated before and after the delivery of feed, and appear to have to been due to feeding for an unnaturally short duration. This was due to the provision of conserved pasture in a single location and because the volume of concentrate required to deliver a specified nutritional benefit may be consumed in a shorter time than would be required to graze sufficient pasture to obtain an equivalent benefit. Outside of the mating period, male bighorn sheep and mountain goats observed over three years in Alberta dedicated 75 percent of their active time to foraging, with much of their lying time spent ruminating.[30] On a heather moorland enclosure of 1.25 square kilometers, in the Scottish Highlands, wild boar monitored with the aid of GPS collars spent 55 percent of their time in summer foraging, with this rising to 80 percent in autumn and winter, even when supplementary feed was provided to ensure adequate nutrition.[31] During winter, rooting predominated, although, in May and June, the prevalence of grazing over rooting bracken and grass reflected the vegetation that was seasonally available.

In the Bible, grazing is the normal method of feeding ruminant animals, providing for both nutritional and behavioral needs in a varied environment in which animals experience a wide range of natural stimuli. Although it is likely to be in the welfare interest

---

27:29.

28. Deut 25:4; 1 Tim 5:18a.

29. Ishiwata et al., "Comparison."

30. Pelletier et al., "Rut-Induced Hypophagia."

31. Sandom et al., "Rewilding."

of these animals to be provided with feed supplements when grazing is limited, and to be moved inside during harsh weather conditions and then fed on conserved forage, these alternatives do not satisfy behavioral needs as fully on an ongoing basis.

3. Migration and Route-Finding

Biblical writers frequently observe, and sometimes commend, the abilities of animal species living in the wild. Some of these species may also be farmed, or possess abilities or physiological features similar to those of farmed species. The prophet Jeremiah cuttingly contrasts the knowledge that migratory bird species display, which displays advanced route-finding abilities, with human ignorance of God's judgment.[32] In the Song of Solomon, the arrival of the migratory turtledove signals the new life of spring.[33] In the Flood narrative, the dove that Noah releases from the ark is able to find its way back.[34] Some bird species certainly have better navigational abilities than humans. Chickens possess a magnetic compass similar to that found in migratory bird species and in carrier pigeons. The mechanism for this used to be thought to be grains of the iron oxide magnetite within their beaks. However, their route-finding ability is now recognized to be due to the blue light receptor cryptochrome 4 (Cry4), and possibly to other retinal proteins, which enable chickens to visualize magnetic fields. In conjunction with their developing knowledge of landmarks, this enables orientation on a range.[35] This is probably important for birds that are unable to fly at height and that, in the wild, typically inhabit areas of ground cover and forest and are thus vulnerable to predation.

Navigational ability is also vital for fish. At the conclusion of Psalm 8, those that pass through the paths of the seas are presented

32. Jer 8:7.
33. Song 2:12.
34. Gen 8:11.
35. Wiltschko et al., "The Magnetic Compass."

as part of the works of God that display divine majesty.[36] *Orachot* is typically used to describe paths or highways that have been purposively defined by individuals, and in this instance suggests directional passage from one location to another along routes that are repeatedly used. Commentators on the Genesis 1 creation narrative justly portray fish migration at length. Basil of Caesarea describes the seasonal movement of fish from the Aegean Sea into the Black Sea, undoubtedly drawing on knowledge of the region in which he lived.[37] Praising fish for knowing the "time to be born,"[38] Ambrose of Milan develops this account, recognizing their migration to be motivated by the need to spawn in water of low salinity. The bishop writes of fish "gathering together, as if with joint purpose" and being "impelled . . . by a law of nature . . . to their familiar haunts."[39] Basil describes fish navigating the Sea of Marmara in order to complete the reverse passage, from the Black Sea into the Aegean Sea, following a sensory mechanism implanted in their senses in accordance with divine law and "celestial mandates." He goes on to argue that this migratory pattern is fundamentally rational, being due both to the Black Sea's low salinity and to the prevailing northerly wind tempering its summer heat. Once spawning is complete, fish return to the Aegean, avoiding the winter turbidity and freezing of the Black Sea that results from storms, and from the inflow of cold water from many large rivers.

Fish behavioral research confirms and extends Ambrose's insights. Brown sea trout spawn in rivers, but may migrate to live in saltwater during the spring and summer, or even until the following year or later, primarily in order to access an improved food supply, and thus to increase body weight gain.[40] Smoltification, which is the set of physical and behavioral changes that prepare

36. Ps 8:8. Many of the occurrences of *orachot* are in Job, Proverbs, and other psalms.

37. Basil, "On the Hexameron" 7.4, 111–13.

38. Eccl 3:2.

39. Ambrose, *Hexameron* 10 (29–30), 183–86. The salinity of the Black Sea is about half that of the Aegean Sea and of oceans.

40. Thorstad et al., "Marine Life."

juveniles for saltwater living, can occur as early as a year old, although, in northerly latitudes with low water temperatures, may be delayed for several seasons. In studies that have included the recapture of tagged trout, migration distance has usually been found to be within eighty kilometers of the river of origin, although, in the Baltic region, distances of over eight hundred kilometers have been recorded.[41] In such studies, most trout are not recovered, which may contribute to a tendency to underestimate the typical distances traversed.

Salmon develop and migrate according to similar principles. However, they travel even further than trout, typically moving several hundred kilometers to feeding grounds, with recapture distances as great as thirteen hundred kilometers being recorded, also in the Baltic region.[42] The navigational methods that salmon employ have been extensively discussed, with several likely to be in use depending on the migratory phase. From a route-finding perspective, outward migration is relatively unsophisticated, although is influenced by wind-driven surface currents, prey distribution, and water temperature. Return homing is controlled with far greater accuracy, with information sources on the open sea potentially including the sun, polarized light, the earth's magnetic field, induced electrical fields, olfactory cues, and the orbital motion of swell detected by the inner ear. As the coast is approached, a combination of current, tide, temperature, salinity, and bodily chemicals that have previously been released, as well as cues recalled from outward migration, allow greater precision, which is needed as the earth's magnetic field patterns slowly but continually shift.[43]

In wild conditions, salmon and brown trout display complex behaviors that, even now, are not fully understood by humans. These are also the fish species that are farmed in greatest numbers in highly restricted conditions in which they are unable to exercise these behaviors. Fish that are caught on open water are likely to

41. Thorstad et al., "Marine Life," 7–9.
42. Kallio-Nyberg and Ikonen, "Migration Pattern," 193–94.
43. Thorpe, "Salmon Migration;" Hansen et al., "Oceanic Migration."

have had the opportunity to express a fuller range of behaviors and abilities than those that have been farmed.

4. Play

It is striking that some spontaneous animal play movements make such an impression on the psalmist that he employs them to depict large-scale movements of landscapes. When used with reference to mountains, the movements of farm animals suggest something similar to an earthquake. The mountains skip (*raqad*) like rams, and Lebanon skips like a calf.[44] Such imagery suggests that play is significant for individual young, and as part of the wider created order. Among lambs, play behaviors are concentrated in the first two months of life. On a wildlife range in Montana, on which their play was studied over a period of twenty-eight months, its repertoire was found to include butting, clashing, threat jumping, presenting, horn threatening, face rubbing, shoulder pushing, low stretching, mounting, twisting, front kicking, head touching, neck wrestling, and neck twisting.[45] Such movements, being playful, have no ulterior purpose, although probably have the effect of promoting physical strength and motor training. Wild sheep are likely to be particularly vulnerable to predation during play periods, due to moving away from adults. Indeed, the danger of predation in such a situation is referred to in the book of Job, in which the mountains "where all the wild animals play" yield food for the beast Behemoth.[46] The fact that play has nevertheless been observed even among wild flocks indicates its great importance for development. Indeed, the benefits of play that have just been described may well hone abilities that ultimately aid self-defense and flight. Older sheep may occasionally be observed playing, including in exceptional bouts involving multiple animals and

44. Pss 114:4, 6; 29:6.
45. Hass and Jenni, "Social Play."
46. Job 40:20 (NRSV).

lasting several minutes.[47] Play in sheep does not appear to promote social cohesion: male lambs are observed playing more frequently than females, even though the flock social structure is built around females.

Among dairy calves, researchers in the Czech Republic observed play behaviors that included running, leaping, jumping, rearing, head jerking, head shaking, buck kicking, fast turning, turning, object play, contact play, butting, mounting, kicking, running together, and leaping or jumping together.[48] Calves that were accommodated in groups of four played more frequently than those confined within individual pens. However, when moved into a social situation with more space, calves that had been confined exhibited a high play level for at least twenty-four hours. These previously confined calves played even more intensively than those that had become accustomed to group accommodation. The extended duration of the play period suggests that it was the result not just of novelty but of built-up motivation during the preceding period of social deprivation. In a study of Holstein calves in British Columbia, the larger the test arena (up to thirty meters long), the greater the amount of play that was observed that involved movement around the arena.[49] Animals were more likely to play when in the arena for the first time, confirming that novelty is a factor inducing play. For young bulls, when animals from a stable herd are brought together, interactions in either play or sparring include pawing, flehmen (curling the upper lip), nosing, and head-pushing. By eighteen months of age, grooming, and especially head-pushing, become a purposeful means of establishing group hierarchy.[50]

For piglets studied in Scotland over four months, play behaviors were classified as scampering, pivoting, head tossing, flopping, hopping, rolling, gambolling, pushing, nudging, chasing, push

47. Hass and Jenni, "Social Play," 111.
48. Valníčková et al., "The Effect."
49. Mintline et al., "Assessing."
50. Hinch et al., "Patterns."

overs, sow climbing, sow nudging, shaking, and carrying.[51] Piglets raised in a free-farrowing environment played more than those within a conventional crate system. In line with other studies of piglets, the main benefits of play were found to be the promotion of group socialization and cognitive development. In piglets, play appears to be less closely related to physical development than in ruminants.

The rich play repertoires of farm animals that have been systematically observed and recorded by researchers provide evidence that endorses the biblical view of animals as having their own lives and modes of flourishing that are independent of human needs. In several places in the Bible, animals are described as praising God.[52] For animals, play seems to represent what such praise entails: the free exercise of created capacities, including vocalization, not for productive purposes but as a celebration of life.

5. Conclusion

Farm animal species exhibit distinctive behaviors from soon after birth. These are closely related to habitat and feeding. Species flourish in different habitats, and some may range over a wide area when nesting and feeding. The soil that is provided by the habitat is important as a growing medium for plants that may be grazed, browsed, or foraged below surface level. Consuming food in this way satisfies an important physiological and behavioral need for all farmed species and is how they spend a large proportion of every day. For chickens, appropriately dry and friable soil also enables dustbathing, which both maintains plumage condition and is a behavioral need.

Some farmed species possess abilities that are far superior to the equivalent capacities in humans. Fish may migrate long distances to access food supplies and temperate waters, before navigating back to a precise freshwater location to spawn. Chickens

51. Martin et al., "The Influence."
52. Pss 148:7–10; 150:6; Pr Azar 57–59. See Atkins, "Praise."

are able to route-find on a range at ground level by visualizing the earth's magnetic field. Other behaviors, which are classified as play, may, in different species, have the effects of aiding physical development, promoting motor skills, or fostering social cohesion. However, from a theological perspective, their principal importance is as an expression of a flourishing life.

4

Stockpersons

IT IS A TRUISM that stockpersons are central to the welfare of farm animals. The stockperson may be the resident farmer or another person charged by the owner of land and farm buildings with exercising the duty of care to animals. On large farms, especially where the farmer or owner is not resident, there will be a farm manager who has responsibility for other farm workers. The stockperson controls access to built and outdoor environments and maintains them. They make decisions about shelter, food, and drink, and provide these. When animals are indoors, they control light, heat, and ventilation levels, or oversee their automated regulation. They take measures to reduce the incidence of injury and disease, and, when these occur, treat or medicate animals themselves, or enlist the help of a veterinary surgeon. They maintain records and report to external bodies, such as an assurance scheme.

The term "stockperson" primarily designates the person in daily charge of farm animals but may, by extension, be used to refer to other workers who share in this responsibility and carry out tasks that contribute to animal care. I use the term in this inclusive sense. This chapter first describes in broad perspective the biblical understanding of farm animals, showing how this supports the objective view of animals on which husbandry rests. It then discusses the importance of the human–animal bond and frames this within a covenantal context. Stockperson behavior and attitudes are next addressed, in the context of empathy and vocation. There follows a consideration of the shifting boundary between maternal, dominant male, and stockperson functions, and of how animals may sometimes regard the stockperson as a herdmate. The chapter ends by considering the changing role of the stockperson, which is a consequence of technological innovation and of increased herd and flock sizes.

1. Human Use of Animals

In the first Genesis creation narrative, it is twice stated that humans are to rule, or to have dominion (*radah*), over all living creatures.[1] The instruction to the Israelites to rule over animals indicates that, unlike members of many other ancient religions, they are not to worship them, nor to view them as sources of power or knowledge. In ancient Hittite religion, it was believed that, by observing the behavior of farm animals, or by examining their entrails, future events could be foretold.[2] In one fertility ritual, women stood over a pig while reciting a creation story. In ancient Mesopotamia, humans frequently sought protection by attempting to harness the spiritual powers that farm animals were thought to possess.[3] A goat, chicken, goose, sheep, or bull might be slaughtered to expel an evil spirit from a person or house—sometimes, in the case of a person, by physical contact with the carcass. By cradling a swaddled dead lamb, or by crawling under a suspended pregnant ewe, a woman might try to avoid a stillbirth.

In practice, some Israelites probably treated animals in ways associated with non-Israelite religions. In the Old Testament, this superstitious relationship with animals is countered by a large and foundational body of teaching that promotes husbandry

---

1. Gen 1:26, 28.
2. Collins, "Animals," 319, 323.
3. Scurlock, "Animals," 374–82, 384–85.

and appropriate use. Dominion thus understood is confirmed by its close association with the making of humans in God's image (*tzelem*) and likeness (*demuth*).[4] The enactment of dominion allied humans with God and, by implication, differentiated animals from God, over whom humans certainly could not exercise dominion. Again, the contrasts with other ancient religions are clear. In ancient Hittite religion, bulls were believed to possess divine power because of their strength.[5] In ancient Egypt, living bulls were worshipped and prayed to.[6] The goddesses Hathor and Mehet-Weret were represented as a cow, while rams, sows, pigs, and geese were believed to represent other gods. Neo-Assyrian art depicts gods riding animals including bulls and a goat-fish.[7] In Syro-Palestinian religions, the preeminent god, Baal, was presented as a bull, notably in King Jeroboam's installation of golden bulls at the shrines he established at Dan and Bethel, when seeking to effect a break with the Jerusalem temple.[8]

In summary, the Genesis creation narratives indicate that humans should deal with animals objectively and should not be spiritually dependent on them. Because human dominion is so closely related to humans bearing God's image and likeness, it should be understood with reference to the *kind of dominion that God exercises*. This substantially corrects common misunderstandings of dominion as excusing, or even as mandating, the human mistreatment of animals. In Genesis 1, God provides for animal needs, commanding that there be light, forming sky, and, on the third day, causing dry land to appear out of the separation of the waters, and commanding that the earth grow (*dasha*) vegetation (*deshe*), which includes plants (*eseb*) yielding seed (*zera*) and trees producing fruit (*peri*). On the sixth day, the produce of the third day, which is made possible by the productive acts of the first and second days, is given to animals, as well as to humans, as food.

4. Gen 1:26, 27; also 5:1; 9:6.

5. Collins, "Animals," 314.

6. Teeter, "Animals," 335–37, 347–48.

7. Scurlock, "Animals," 361–62.

8. Borowski, "Animals," 407–8, 412; 1 Kgs 7:25.

God is thus shown to be fundamentally a provider of light, habitat, water, and food. This is in sharp contrast with many non-Israelite conceptions of God. In the creation narratives of ancient Mesopotamia, humans are created to supply food to gods, following shortages due to the increased number of gods that have been the progeny of divine marriages, and to the disinclination of the lower gods to undertake this demanding service.[9] In Mesopotamia, gods were hungry, requiring twice daily feeding on a meat-based diet.[10] In Genesis, the direction of giver and gift is reversed: God does not require food, but is the supplier of food.

The nature of humans' relationship with animals may be further understood with reference to other Old Testament descriptions of dominion. Although the majority of these include elements of force, or of governance by means of power over unwilling subjects, exceptions are identifiable. These suggest that, although human rule is often in reality grounded in the willed subjugation of the ruled, this is not necessarily the case, and potentially should not be the case. In Leviticus, God instructs the Israelites that the rule (*radah*) that they exercise over their dependents, slaves, and resident aliens should not be harsh.[11] The wise King Solomon of Israel rules (*radah*) over a wide territory, with his officers exercising authority (*radah*).[12] A liturgical usage is also noteworthy: in the Psalms, the tribe of Benjamin, which stems from the youngest of Jacob's offspring, leads (*radah*) the procession into the sanctuary.[13] This suggests that truly holy rule (*hier-arkhia*) entails an inversion of the normal order of precedence and status. Such an inversion is evidenced in the work of the good stockperson, who consistently exercises care for their animals in sometimes physically difficult conditions or at times of the day, week, and year that disrupt family life and social life. A good life for animals is enabled by stockpersons who exercise power responsibly and even sacrificially.

9. Lambert, *Ancient Mesopotamian Religion*, 171–79.

10. Scurlock, "Animal Sacrifice."

11. Lev 25:43, 46, 53.

12. 1 Kgs 4:24; Ps 72:8; 2 Chr 8:10.

13. Ps 68:27.

2. The Human–Animal Relationship

Within the Judeo-Christian tradition, the domestication of animals for human production entails the "unspiritual" and objective view of animals just outlined. This enables appropriate confinement within fields or buildings, and permits watering, feeding, handling, medical interventions, transportation, and slaughter. However, in the Judeo-Christian tradition a deep relationality between humans and animals is also recognized. This is literally grounded on the making of livestock and humans together on the sixth day of creation to inhabit the dry land that was made to appear on the third day.[14]

Allowing the human–animal relationship to shape stockperson treatment of animals is likely to improve the lives of both animals and stockpersons.[15] For animals, the welfare benefits of a strong bond with the stockperson include increased comfort due to their needs easily being met, calmer behavior as fearful responses are minimized, and life-enrichment gained through interaction with a different sentient species. Furthermore, the easier handling and management that a strong bond is likely to bring may reduce the need for measures such as disbudding. Frequent close contact enables the early detection and treatment of disease or injury. The continuation of an animal's life may depend on stockperson intervention, for example, when a lamb (such as a twin) is lost, abandoned, or attacked by their dam, or the dam is unable to sustain it, or dies after giving birth.[16] For the stockperson, wellbeing may be increased by the easier and safer performance of husbandry tasks, the companionship of one or more other sentient species, and an improved psychological state.

The human–animal bond exists within a social context. Humans typically live in groups and most farm animal species form herds or flocks. Rather than viewing humans and farm animals as two distinct but overlapping communities, it may be preferable

14. Gen 1:24–26. See Grumett, "Food."
15. Anthony, "The Ethical Implications," 507.
16. Grubb, "Social Organization," 142–43.

to regard them as a single community. In historical perspective, most communities have comprised both humans and animals. Humans have raised animals for their meat, milk, wool, hair, and other products in both nomadic and settled contexts. The extremely small number of species that humans have domesticated for farming purposes are each inherently social and are inclined to hierarchical group organization. Humans have therefore been able to enter into their social life and change it. Farm animals have even inspired human naming: Rachel (*rahel*) is the Hebrew term for a ewe, while Rebecca (*ribqah*) describes a group of animals tied together for a purpose such as milking.[17] Across many cultures, there is evidence that humans and farm animals have shared accommodation, at least during winter. In ancient Israel, four-room houses with two storeys included ground-floor space for storage, for workspace, and, in rural areas, for sheltering animals, which helped to raise the temperature of the rooms on the upper floor immediately above them. Arranged with the ground floor divided into a central entrance hall and separate rooms leading off this on either side, and at the end, these houses enabled access to one room without passing through others, and so aided the observance of purity laws.[18] In some regions of Britain, longhouses accommodated humans and livestock in comparably close proximity.

Humans have benefitted from this shared socialization by gaining access to meat, dairy products, and fibre, while, from an evolutionary perspective, farmed species have adapted from living in the wild, and have thereby increased their genetic fitness by benefitting from the food, water, shelter, and protection that are delivered by husbandry.[19] Farm animals and humans may communicate, with stockpersons frequently using speech when dealing with their animals, even on occasions when no other human is present. In John's Gospel, Jesus's comparison of his followers with the sheep of a shepherd who hear his voice and follow him suggests

---

17. Borowski, *Every Living Thing*, 44.
18. Bunimovitz and Faust, "Building Identity."
19. Stricklin, "Evolution."

that sheep may recognize the voice of an individual stockperson.[20] Both humans and animals deploy facial expression and other body language. Animals may, for their part, be cooperative or disruptive, employ intelligence to solve problems, adapt to physical constraints, and push system boundaries. Humans and animals share the benefits and costs of the farming environment and conditions. Requiring farm workers to perform tasks unrealistically quickly is likely to increase human stress and to reduce the attention paid to animals, whereas allowing more time to complete jobs allows them to enjoy being with animals and aids the early diagnosis and treatment of injury or disease. Zoonotic disease, including respiratory infections and other viruses, may spread both from humans to animals and from animals to humans.[21]

Animals have even been viewed as coworkers with humans in purposeful productive activity, occupying a common workspace and interacting with the stockperson both directly and via machinery.[22] Like humans, they may sometimes choose not to work or to be less productive. This image of the animal as worker is especially appropriate for milking cows and laying hens, which regularly produce items for human consumption.

One way of understanding the human–animal bond in farming is as a contract.[23] According to this view, some animal species give up their freedom to exist in the wild in order to benefit from human husbandry. They are not required to surrender the whole of their freedom, but only as much as is necessary in order to gain particular benefits. The problems with contractualism in the context of human–animal community are similar to, although are no greater than, those identified by political theorists in relation to human political community. No point in history may be identified

20. John 10:27. The hypothesis that a sheep is able to recognize a voice that it has heard as belonging to a particular known human has not been confirmed by research. Among sheep, the facial identification of humans is likely to be more important than vocal recognition. See Kendrick et al., "Facial and Vocal Discrimination."

21. Porcher, "The Relationship."

22. Porcher and Schmitt, "Dairy Cows."

23. Larrère and Larrère, "Animal Rearing."

when the supposed contract was enacted, and the notion of a contract assumes free agents able to communicate, and potentially to opt out. The human–animal bond may be better framed as the product of a covenant, which, like a contract, imposes entitlements and responsibilities on the parties to it. However, whereas a contract is enacted between purportedly free and equal individuals on their own terms, in the Old Testament, covenants were given by God and were unconditional and everlasting.[24] The God of the Old Testament remained faithful to his people. In modern farming settings, the levels of authority and power that humans have over animals are similar to those that the ancient Israelites viewed God as having over them. A covenantal perspective suggests a continuing obligation on humans, regardless of the perceived norms of farming in a particular place and at a given time, to treat animals well. Just as God has been faithful to humans, so humans should keep faith with farm animals.

In Genesis, the Noahic covenant, which is never abrogated, explicitly includes both humans and animals. In the Flood narrative, Noah and his family are stockpersons who construct a safe built environment for domesticated species and other animals, gather them into it, and exercise a duty of care toward them, before returning them to their outdoor environment.[25] As a result of the Flood, all farm animal species outside of this built environment, and without human husbandry, perish. Given that Noah and his family function as stockpersons, it is unsurprising that the covenant that God promises to Noah, and later establishes with him, includes domesticated animals (*behemah*).[26] Rather than invoking a harmonious human–animal relationship as a future promise, it presents such a relationship as possible, and indeed as required, in the present, with the requirements that follow from it being

24. Hiuser and Barton, "A Promise." There is some similarity with a covenant in property law, which imposes obligations on future owners of land or of a building who were not originally party to it.

25. Gen 6:11—8:19.

26. Gen 6:18; 9:10. See Murray, *The Cosmic Covenant*, 32–35.

enforceable by law.[27] These requirements are not detailed in the narrative but appear through the first five books of the Old Testament.

3. Behavior and Attitudes

Stockperson behavior has a fundamental impact on farm animal welfare, especially in farming systems such as dairy that require frequent interaction between stockpersons and animals. Yet it varies widely. It may be viewed as a function of personality and attitude. Psychologists typically regard personality as the ongoing foundation of character, which is stable from mature adulthood, whereas attitude is related to context, and is changeable. A study of dairy farmers in Northern Ireland examined the contributions of personality and attitude to welfare. The relative importance in respondents of each of the key personality traits of extraversion, agreeableness, conscientiousness, emotional stability, and intellect was measured using a standard fifty-item questionnaire.[28] An accompanying questionnaire, which was carefully constructed and trialed, assessed respondents against the attitudes of empathy, negative beliefs, job satisfaction, and patience, as measured via answers to forty-two questions about aspects of cow welfare and handling. Milk yield, controlled for external factors, was used as an indicator of welfare, on the reasonable grounds that high welfare increases production.[29] This was a demanding means of quantifying the stockperson contribution to welfare, given that yield is a function of a range of variables, of which welfare is unlikely to be the most important. The findings suggested that personality alone has little impact on welfare, but that the attitudes of empathy and

27. VanDrunen, *Divine Covenants*, 95–132, especially 115–23.

28. Hanna et al. "The Relationship." A study using the same methodology was later conducted in Japan with similar findings: Fukasawa et al., "Relationship."

29. This does not mean that high productivity always entails high welfare nor that productivity gains are always due to welfare gains.

job satisfaction that it produces, principally via agreeableness and conscientiousness, are significant.

Attitudes have some similarity with virtues, being internalized by the individual and therefore requiring self-reflection. This suggests that self-awareness, not just technical training, is vital for stockpersons. Self-awareness may be promoted by reflection on one's own behavior and its impact on animals. The qualitative behavioral assessment of stockpersons in charge of calves has been used to examine the relationship between handling styles and animal behavior.[30] Stockperson behavior characterized by calmness and patience, and especially by positive interactions with animals, was correlated with positive calf mood, including friendliness, contentment, and sociability. In contrast, stockpersons who were classed as insecure and nervous, or as dominant and aggressive, were associated with higher incidences of negative calf mood, evidenced by features such as nervousness, frustration, and fear.

Attitudes are contextual, being assessed, as in the study just discussed, by conduct in a role. This suggests that Christian ethics, which is concerned with both general principles of conduct, and with behavior in specific settings, may positively contribute to farm animal welfare. Regarding the attitude of empathy, John's Gospel presents the powerful image of Jesus the good shepherd knowing (*ginosko*) his sheep.[31] Although Jesus is obviously male, the type of knowing here being identified is by no means limited to men. Rachel was a shepherd, meeting Jacob, whom she would later wed, while watering her father Laban's sheep.[32] The seven daughters of the priest Jethro were shepherds. These included Zipporah, who became the wife of Moses after their encounter at his intervention in support of the daughters, during a water dispute with shepherds in Egypt.[33] Rebecca, who became the wife of Isaac, was also involved in the care of animals, drawing water for them, and

---

30. Ellingsen et al., "Using Qualitative Behaviour Assessment."

31. John 10:14, 27. For background, Borowski, *Every Living Thing*, 48–50.

32. Gen 29:4–10.

33. Exod 2:16–19.

having charge of bedding and feed.[34] In the New Testament, on most of the occasions when women are present at a well to collect water, the intended use of this water is unspecified. It is reasonable to suppose that, in many instances, the water being collected is for domesticated animals.

The tremendous importance and value of the kind of knowledge associated with shepherding, whether undertaken by men or by women, is underlined in the description of David as the shepherd and ruler of Israel. This designation is echoed in the response of the chief priests and scribes to King Herod immediately following Jesus's birth, that out of Bethlehem will "come a ruler who is to shepherd my people Israel."[35] Such knowledge includes several features, including: (i) intimacy; (ii) an intuitive grasp of situations; (iii) the correct perception of circumstantial facts that are not immediately apparent; and (iv) the appraisal of the significance of information and events.[36] All these contribute to empathy, which involves a degree of feeling for another sentient being, the imaginative leap that is needed to identify and consider the kinds of emotions that it might be experiencing, and the prudence to take effective action. From a Christian perspective, empathy is exemplified in Jesus, who combines the human ability to feel with the divine purity that is receptive of others to the point of suffering and even death. In Jesus, empathy is shown in love, compassion, and sympathy, which evoke responses, and thereby incorporate the other within a cooperative union.[37] Empathy is thus active and efficacious, expanding the circle of concern beyond its normal objects. This theological understanding of empathy is consistent with the empirical finding that humans empathize with farm animal species.[38]

34. Gen 24:19–20, 25.

35. 2 Sam 5:2; Matt 2:6b (NRSV).

36. (i) Matt 1:25; Luke 1:34; 21:30–31; John 14:17; (ii) John 2:25; 6:15; 8:32; 16:19; (iii) Luke 8:10, 17; 18:34; 24:35; (iv) Matt 24:32–33; Mark 13:28–29; John 12:16.

37. Farley, *Divine Empathy*, 295–96, 303–5.

38. For the latter, see also Burton et al., "Building 'Cowshed Cultures.'"

The job satisfaction of stockpersons is frequently low, due to factors such as working conditions and hours, perceived low occupational status, and low pay.[39] The perception of the value of work as a stockperson may be greatly enhanced by interpreting it, in Christian terms, as a vocation or calling. It might be supposed that only monks, nuns, and clergy, and perhaps those working in a few other select professions such as medicine and teaching, may be said to possess a vocation. However, this supposition was called fundamentally into question at the Protestant Reformation by Martin Luther. An example of vocation from Luther is that of a farmworker. While relating the story of Jacob and Laban, the Reformer affirms, in terms that were theologically and politically contentious: "God's people please God even in the least and most trifling matters. For He will be working all things through you; He will milk the cow through you and perform the most servile duties through you, and all the greatest and least duties alike will be pleasing to Him."[40] When celebrating the humility of Mary the mother of Jesus, the first of her household chores that Luther enumerates is milking cows. He also describes the milking of goats as pleasing to God.

Empirical research confirms that the concept of vocation is applicable to far more occupations than just the religious and professional. If a vocation makes reference to God, who presides over the whole of the created world, it seems unjustified to regard only a small number of occupations as vocational. Because vocation is inherently personal, the self-reporting by practitioners of how they understand their role is highly relevant. In a major qualitative survey of North American zookeepers, most viewed their work vocationally, believing that their gifts and opportunities had drawn them to this occupation, and no other.[41] The zookeepers regarded their work as binding and ennobling, but also as a moral

39. Hemsworth and Coleman, *Human–Livestock Interactions*, 2, 5–6.

40. Martin Luther, *Commentary on Genesis* 31.1.3, translated by Paul D. Pahl, in Luther, *Works* 6.10; also *The Magnificat (Lk. 1.49)*, in *Works*, 21.329; *Commentary on Genesis* 29.1.13, in *Works*, 5.284–85.

41. Bunderson and Thompson, "The Call."

duty entailing some personal sacrifice in order to maintain high standards and avoid poor welfare. They strongly believed in the objective importance of their work for society and the world.

Although zookeepers typically hold a higher level of educational qualification than stockpersons, and work within a visitor environment, the roles are sufficiently equivalent for there to be similarities in self-understanding. Viewing stockmanship as a vocation gives a meaning and value to the tasks performed that they might otherwise be felt to lack. It is to recognize that stockmanship is a role to which some are called that has an intrinsic value equal to that of any other occupation and that is greater than the value of roles that are performed for non-vocational objectives such as personal gain or public praise. This does not, however, require an uncritical acceptance of existing practices and traditions. When viewing their work vocationally, stockpersons set it within the larger contexts of God's will for the world and the gifts they have been given. These may well entail a constructively critical approach to daily practice and its underpinning assumptions.

Personality and attitudes are formed in social contexts, which are, in turn, shaped by the built environment.[42] Because farmers often lack the funds needed to invest in new or renovated buildings, farm animal accommodation is frequently outdated, with its design failing to take account of understanding gained from advances in welfare science. Building design should aid the flow of animals, such as by a wide funnel at the opening of races (walkways), which should be curved, and should have boarded sides to prevent animals from being startled by outside movements. Without such features, animals will be harder to manage, with greater risk of injury to both animals and stockpersons, which, over time, is likely to have a negative effect on animal welfare and stockperson attitude. Similarly, the cow tracks that are used by grazed dairy herds when walking to and from the milking parlor are a significant investment and need to be well-designed and maintained. If they are not, the incidence of lameness is likely to increase, and it will be harder for stockpersons to move animals. This may lead to

42. Burton et al., "Building 'Cowshed Cultures.'"

the increased use of sticks or goads and have a negative effect on stockperson attitude over time.

4. Stockpersons as Animals

Within animal farming settings, humans support, or perform, roles that would otherwise be carried out by herdmates or flockmates. Most basically, they protect group members from predators. Stockpersons frequently provide young with warmth, colostrum, milk, and physical contact. This by no means excludes the robust, and even aggressive, treatment of animals when the occasion demands. In some nomadic cultures, herders consciously imitate the behavior of dominant animals in order to control the group, such as by aggressively brandishing a herding stick at a bull, shouting at it, and charging, in order to assert their own superior dominance.[43] Such interventions may, for example, break up fights, or protect unenclosed crops. In more usual circumstances, farm animals may respond to stockpersons by displaying licking or play interest. Moreover, male animals, including kids, lambs, and piglets, that are isolated from herdmates, are likely to develop sexual interest in stockpersons.[44] On grounds such as these, it may be argued that farmed species relate to their stockpersons as a herdmates.[45] Such relationships need not be direct: by developing positive relationships with dominant or leader animals, which may exercise a mediating function between the stockperson and other herd members, the stockperson influences the behavior of these other animals.

Farm animal attachment to stockpersons has been shown to be increased by periodic direct feeding and petting in early life, with the fear of stockpersons correspondingly reduced. In such situations, the stockperson effectively takes the place of the dam. For instance, in experimental conditions, ewe lambs were separated

43. Lott and Hart, "Applied Ethology."
44. Sambraus and Sambraus, "Prägung."
45. Boivin et al., "Stockmanship," 486–87.

from their dams and fed from teat buckets for their first two days of life, then placed into three groups for four weeks.[46] During this period, one group received no further human contact, the second was stroked by a stockperson, and the third was both stroked and fed. In four tests performed over the following two months, the lambs that had been stroked and fed chose to spend the most time with the human, followed by those that had only been stroked, with those that had been neither stroked nor fed spending the least time. Moreover, when in the presence of the human, the lambs that had been neither stroked nor fed vocalized more frequently than those from the other two groups, suggesting a degree of fear of the human. In contrast, the lambs that vocalized the most when the human departed, which suggests fear at the prospect of separation from the human, were those that during the earlier four-week period had been both stroked and fed. This suggests that early lamb interactions with a stockperson provide the basis for an enduring bond. In a comparable experiment conducted with cattle, bucket-reared calves were fed and handled by humans over three different four-day periods during their first two weeks of life, but otherwise had little human interaction.[47] A control group had no human contact. In three tests during the following two months, the calves that had been fed and handled during the first four days of life were the quickest to interact with a human and were more likely to approach and face them. Moreover, when a human came near, the control group had the longest flight distance. These findings indicate that, as with lambs, early calf handling and feeding help to establish a human–animal relationship. In cattle, the effect of early touching has been shown to persist through an animal's life, whereas introducing this later has far less impact.[48]

If a farm animal builds a strong relationship with a human, its experience of the maternal bond is likely to be weakened. In another experiment, ten pairs of twin lambs were separated from their dam soon after birth. During its first four days of life, one

46. Boivin et al., "Hand-Feeding."
47. Krohn et al., "The Effect."
48. Probst et al., "Gentle Touching;" cf. Probst, "Influence."

member of each pair was then periodically separated from its twin by a wire fence, and was handled and fed by a human, while the other member of the pair had no human contact.[49] Another ten pairs of twin lambs were kept with their dam. One member of each pair was periodically separated from her, handled, and fed, while the other was isolated. By the end of the experiment, the lambs that had been separated from their dam soon after birth were far more likely to accept human contact and feeding than those that had not, including those that had nevertheless received identical human contact and feeding in addition to maternal care. This suggests that maternal care is likely to limit the development of the bond between a lamb and a stockperson. Moreover, in a preference test, most of the lambs that had been separated from their dam soon after birth, and had received periodic human contact, chose to spend time with the familiar human, despite the relatively short time periods that had previously been spent with them, rather than to spend time with an unfamiliar human. This indicates that lambs just a few days old can discriminate between individual humans. Lastly, this same group of lambs vocalized and walked much less when in the presence of the familiar human than when with the unfamiliar human, suggesting that they were more at ease in familiar human company. Similar patterns have been identified in calves. In three tests conducted during the first two months of life, calves that had previously been reared separately from their dam interacted with a human far more quickly than calves that had remained with, or adjacent to, their dam, including a group that had also received human handling and feeding.[50] This greater willingness to interact with a human was found among calves separated from their dam at birth and those separated after four days. This suggests that, with calves, the physical presence and licking of the dam, even when suckling is prevented, impedes the development of a strong bond with a stockperson.

The experiments just described use maternal separation, which raises ethical issues about the appropriate balance between

49. Boivin et al., "The Presence."
50. Krohn et al., "The Presence."

stockperson and maternal care and about the freedom of choice about this balance that is available to both the dam and her young. It could be argued that it is preferable, where possible, for an animal to be reared by its own dam rather than by another female of its own species, a female of another species, or a human stockperson. However, the possibility that individual animals may develop a close bond with individual humans suggests that relationships are not intrinsically limited by species. There are also important differences between species. Cows usually produce just one calf per pregnancy, while most sheep breeds average approximately two lambs per litter. Because of the low number of young per dam, a close relationship is likely to exist between the young and dam immediately after a birth. Pig litter sizes, in contrast, have always been larger and, as a result of breeding, for many breeds now average approximately eleven. For this reason, sows do not develop a close bond with their young, tending not to lick individual offspring, nor to help them feed, even though sows may recognize them. For piglets, touching or feeding-support offered by a stockperson is therefore unlikely to duplicate, or to compete with, maternal care, and so is potentially valuable for welfare. In one study, piglets from multiple litters were removed from their dam once a day between their second and fifth weeks of life and stroked for two minutes.[51] In tests undertaken toward the end of the experimental period, those that had been stroked by a human allowed greater human physical contact and vocalized less. In order to achieve this result, it was unnecessary to separate the piglet from their dam.

The notion that the stockperson may be classed as a herd-mate qualifies the human–animal separation that was presented in chapter 4.1 as an essential condition for husbandry. Such blurring of species boundaries between humans and farm animals is identifiable in the Bible. Rebecca places skin from goat kids onto the hands of her son Jacob, who has smooth skin, in order to cause her blind husband Isaac wrongly to believe, on touching Jacob's hands,

---

51. Oliveira et al., "Early Human Handling."

that Jacob is his hairy brother Esau.[52] The deception succeeds, and Isaac gives his blessing to Jacob, who goes on to produce twelve sons, with whom the twelve tribes of Israel are identified. Skinning a dead kid, lamb, or calf and placing the skin onto a living herdmate is the classic, and probably the most reliable, way of grafting an orphan onto a ewe, cow, or doe for feeding and related maternal care. It is thus due to the use of a farm animal husbandry practice on a human, and to the human in this sense becoming an animal, that the structure of Israel, which was based on twelve tribes, was established. In the New Testament, the enumeration of twelve apostles, who gain responsibility for the nascent Christian church and its mission, reflects this history. The functions of ministry are also portrayed using images from animal farming that are based on the interchangeability of human and animal caring functions. Jesus expresses the desire to gather the children of Jerusalem as a hen gathers her chicks (*nossion*) under her wings, and commands Peter to feed his lambs (*arnion*), and to tend his sheep (*probata*).[53]

Nevertheless, the notion that stockpersons may legitimately shape domesticated animal behavior by entering into community with such animals calls into question the notion that there is a fixed set of natural behaviors that a good stockperson should recognize and promote. Stockperson intervention to shape features of animal life that are significant for production far predates modernity. For example, in southern France from the later Neolithic period, moist yet warm autumns that promoted pasture regrowth following summer droughts enabled autumn lambing.[54] This was managed by the separation of ewes and rams by stockpersons and selection for the breeding of autumn offspring. In conjunction with additional fodder provision, and alongside traditional early spring calving, this helped to make sheep products available throughout the year. In research partly informed by work on human–primate communication and language, the philosopher Pär Segerdahl argues that an animal farm should be regarded as a single culture comprising

52. Gen 27:11–23.
53. Matt 23:37; Luke 13:34; John 21:15–16.
54. Tornero et al., "Early Evidence."

the stockpersons and the one or more animal species living on it.[55] Stockpersons shape animal desires and behaviors, which become quickly normalized by means of intergenerational transmission. Moreover, as has already been seen in chapter 4.3, animal behavior contributes to stockperson attitudes, which are likely to spread through existing and incoming farm staff by socialization.

5. The Changing Role of the Stockperson

For most farm animal species, farming systems are evolving in ways that are reducing the necessity and frequency of direct stockperson interactions with animals. For pigs, chickens, and turkeys that are housed indoors, watering is likely to be via an automated nipple and/or cup system, and feeding might also be automated, with ration delivered by a transportation system from large storage bins to a weigher and mixer and, from there, into feeder pans. The primary reason that a stockperson walks a broiler barn is not to care for birds, but to deal with those that are dead or dying. Cleaning may well be automated, such as by mechanical scrapers in a cattle or pig barn, or with slatted concrete floors allowing animals stocked at a sufficiently high density to tread waste down into a storage tank beneath. On dairy farms, rotary milking, in which up to a hundred cows stand facing inwards on a large slowly rotating turntable, reduces the human contact possible in herringbone systems, in which typically two milkers walk between two rows of about twenty cows each facing diagonally outwards, physically checking them. Moreover, some dairy farmers have invested in milking robots, which cows may enter and use without any human assistance, and which monitor individual animals via a microchip on their collar. If an animal declines to vacate the robot after milking, the robot applies an electric shock to expedite exit.[56] Animal movement around built environments may be controlled by automated gates, with individuals similarly identified and granted

55. Segerdahl, "Can Natural Behaviour Be Cultivated?"

56. For this and what follows, see Grumett and Butterworth, "Electric Shock Control."

appropriate access depending on milking, feeding, and medical treatment requirements. Automation is also taking place outdoors. Pasture samples may be analyzed using software. Intensively grazed cattle may be managed by mobile electric fencing that is gradually moved by a robot at each end to permit controlled access to fresh pasture. Electric collars are now commercially available that are designed to achieve the same objective by emitting a warning sound, and then, if necessary, delivering an electric shock to any animal that crosses the virtual boundary. On upland sheep farms, animals may be microchipped to facilitate tracking, which is useful for managing larger herds grazing at a distance from stockpersons.

These shifts in husbandry methods reduce the opportunities for animals and stockpersons to bond. Indeed, on large and highly automated farms, animals may rarely see humans except on highly stressful occasions, such as injections, castration, other mutilations, and the separation of young from their dam.[57] For animals, negative interactions with stockpersons probably have stronger associations than positive interactions, with animals being subsequently likely to fear humans, and to find contact with them stressful. Alongside automation, increasing scale has contributed to this shift. Although, in large herds, positive relationships between animals and stockpersons are possible, they are rarer. For instance, in a study of Swiss and German dairy cattle, the animals in larger herds showed a reduced willingness to be touched due to a lower frequency of direct positive interactions with stockpersons.[58] However, in the largest herd of ninety-two cows, positive interactions had been maintained, and animals were approachable due to the stockperson's herd knowledge and handling style.

Automation is changing the skills required of stockpersons. Both indoors and outdoors, increasing volumes of electronic data on water and feed intake, weight, disease, and productivity are available to aid decision-making. Such monitoring may identify problems earlier than even an experienced stockperson, such as by

57. Tallet et al., "Pig–Human Interactions."
58. Waiblinger and Menke, "Influence."

registering a disease risk by means of the chemical analysis of expressed milk. Within an indoor system, early warning of a potential problem may well be valuable, because disease can spread rapidly. However, there is a danger that information will not be acted on with sufficient speed, or that signs that are observable by an experienced stockperson who has frequent contact with animals will be missed. In well-designed facilities, automation is likely to reduce the distress to animals resulting from poor handling, although, by reducing the frequency, duration, and confidence of stockperson interaction with animals, is also likely to make handling more distressing on the occasions when it is necessary. On sheep and cattle farms where animals are widely dispersed, increased herd size is likely to result in less time being available to a stockperson to check individual animals for disease or injury, such as lameness, which is difficult to identify by remote tracking, unless an animal's condition is so serious that it has become immobile.[59] Moreover, lamb mortality increases if lambing is not subject to direct human supervision.

Many aspects of the stockperson's changing role are economically driven. Farming has always had an economic context, even when undertaken solely for feeding the farmer and their household. Buying or renting land, buying feed, maintaining indoor and outdoor accommodation, and purchasing and servicing equipment, contribute to a farm's regular outgoings. Automating production and increasing scale are ways in which farmers might attempt to reduce costs per production unit. However, on larger farms, the risk of disease spread is likely to be greater, and so careful management, probably with specialized veterinary support, will probably be needed. On almost all farms, veterinary assistance is focused on herd health rather than on individual health. This is because, excepting valuable breeding males and some cattle, the cost of treating individuals is likely to be prohibitively high, relative to the return from the slaughtered carcass or ongoing production. In many countries, animal farming is heavily supported by

59. Stafford and Gregory, "Implications," 276.

government payments, because it preserves the natural environment for human use and enjoyment.

6. Conclusion

The objective view of animals that is presented in the Bible remains fundamental to stockperson attitudes, enabling animals to be farmed for their meat and secondary products under responsible husbandry. Nonetheless, stockpersons live alongside farm animal species in a community with them. The biblical model of shepherding, and the post-Reformation understanding of secular vocation, each contribute to an appropriately high theological valuation of stockpersons and their skills, within a suitable physical environment. Stockpersons may shape animal behavior, especially during the early weeks of life, including by performing functions that might otherwise be undertaken by either the dam, or by a dominant male group member, and have been altering herd dynamics to suit human purposes for millennia. New management and information technologies, and their increasing use, have the potential to improve some aspects of welfare, although, by reducing the frequency of contact between animals and stockpersons, may lead to a loosening of the human–animal bond, and to reduced attention to other areas of welfare.

Epilogue

THE PRECEDING CHAPTERS SUGGEST that the Bible has greater significance for farm animal welfare than is typically supposed. It has been shown that, in the Bible and in theological reflection that draws on it, farm animals are a key part of the natural order created by God and that their characteristic habitats and diet are recognized and provided. Bodily integrity and behavior are similarly respected. Farm animals are viewed not merely in terms of their use value to humans, but as beings with their own intrinsic place in the world. A complex ecology of relation between humans and farm animals is presented that is highly instructive for understanding their relation today, and that calls into question some commonly held assumptions about species boundaries.

The question remains of what may be done today to improve farm animal welfare, and how. Several levers for improvement may be identified. In democratic countries, citizens participate in periodic elections in which they choose political representatives to legislate and to govern. The manifestoes and position statements of candidates standing for election may be scrutinized for commitments relating to animal farming in general and to animal welfare specifically. Within some jurisdictions, citizens may also themselves act directly as legislators by means of initiatives, referenda, or plebiscites. These are bringing about significant animal welfare improvements in some parts of the United States.

Of course, farmers and farm business operators may initiate welfare improvements that go beyond baseline legal and regulatory requirements. They may choose to benchmark and communicate the level of animal welfare that they provide by joining a farm assurance scheme, which has defined standards for particular farm animal species. The formal requirements of a major national retailer may also provide a set of standards. For farms that sell to local retailers, the direct visibility of animals, and the importance of reputation, may have the effect of promoting welfare. In any case, for increasing numbers of farmers and farm businesses, an important future economic driver is likely to be ethical sustainability. Opinions about what is ethically acceptable can rapidly shift. In view of the economic, technological, and planning challenges of altering the systems within which animals are farmed, it would be prudent for those farm businesses that currently provide lower welfare to plan for, and to begin to implement, change now.

Within these political, legislative, business, and regulatory systems, the choices made by consumers are key. Everybody who purchases animal products should inform themselves of the conditions in which the animals whose products they purchase have been reared and should understand the level of welfare that these deliver. For supermarkets, information provided on product packaging and in store is likely to be useful and is variable between countries. There is considerable potential for the increased use of digital technology, such as quick-response codes scanned by smartphones, to provide more information than can be fitted onto packaging.

It is sometimes suggested that global trade acts as a major constraint on farm animal welfare improvements. If minimum standards are raised in one country, so it is suggested, this is likely to result in a price increase to consumers. The result will be, so the argument goes, that products will be imported from locations with even lower welfare requirements, with the net level of farm animal welfare remaining the same, or even falling. However, notwithstanding these considerations, legislators, governments, citizens, farmers, farm business operators, retailers, and consumers are responsible for the welfare of the animals within their own jurisdictions, and which they farm or use.

The Bible and animal welfare research both suggest that the level of welfare that farm animals experience is the product of a range of factors. Some, such as diet, are under direct human control, whereas others are natural, but are able to be mitigated by human intervention. For instance, the effects of adverse weather conditions may be reduced by the provision of shelter. In the Bible, because humans and farm animals live in close proximity, in a situation of mutual dependence that is in accordance with the natural order, the welfare of farm animals can, and should, be protected and promoted. Today this may be done by applying biblical principles informed by modern animal welfare science.

Bibliography

Ambrose. *Hexameron*. Translated by John J. Savage. Fathers of the Church 42. New York: Fathers of the Church, 1961.

Animal Welfare Committee. *Opinion on the Welfare of Cattle Kept in Different Production Systems*. London, 2021.

Anthony, R. "The Ethical Implications of the Human–Animal Bond on the Farm." *Animal Welfare* 12 (2003) 505–12.

Atkins, Peter J. "Praise by Animals in the Hebrew Bible." *Journal for the Study of the Old Testament* 44 (2020) 500–513.

Augustine. *De Doctrina Christiana*. Translated by R. P. H. Green. Oxford: Clarendon, 1995.

Basil of Caesarea. "On the Hexameron." In *Exegetic Homilies*, translated by Sister Agnes Clare Way, 135–50. Fathers of the Church 46. Washington, DC: Catholic University of America Press, 1963.

———. "A Psalm of David at the Finishing of the Tabernacle." In *Exegetic Homilies*, translated by Sister Agnes Clare Way, 193–211. Fathers of the Church 46. Washington, DC: Catholic University of America Press, 1963.

Bates, Ronald O., Mark D. Hoge, David B. Edwards, and Barbara E. Straw. "The Influence of Canine Teeth Clipping on Nursing and Nursery Pig Performance." *Journal of Swine Health and Production* 11 (2003) 75–79.

Berardinelli, J. G., and S. A. Tauck. "Intensity of the Biostimulatory Effect of Bulls on Resumption of Ovulatory Activity in Primiparous, Suckled, Beef Cows." *Animal Reproduction Science* 99 (2007) 24–33.

Berger, Joel. "Facilitation of Reproductive Synchrony by Gestation Adjustment in Gregarious Mammals: A New Hypothesis." *Ecology* 73 (1992) 323–29.

Bertolini, Francesca, Giuseppina Schiavo, Silvia Tinarelli, Laura Santoro, Valerio Joe Utzeri, Stefania Dall'Olio, Leonardo Nanni Costa, Maurizio Gallo, and Luca Fontanesi. "Exploiting Phenotype Diversity in a Local Animal Genetic Resource: Identification of a Single Nucleotide Polymorphism associated with the Tail Shape Phenotype in the Autochthonous Casertana Pig Breed." *Livestock Science* 216 (2018) 148–52.

Blackshaw, Judith K., Alan W. Blackshaw, and John J. McGlone. "Buller Steer Syndrome Review." *Applied Animal Behaviour Science* 54 (1997) 97–108.

Bibliography

Boivin, X., J. Lensink, C. Tallet, and I. Veissier. "Stockmanship and Farm Animal Welfare." *Animal Welfare* 12 (2003) 479–92.

Boivin, X., R. Nowak, and A. Terrazas Garcia. "The Presence of the Dam Affects the Efficiency of Gentling and Feeding on the Early Establishment of the Stockperson–Lamb Relationship." *Applied Animal Behaviour Science* 72 (2001) 89–103.

Boivin, X., H. Tournadre, and P. Le Neindre. "Hand-Feeding and Gentling Influence Early-Weaned Lambs' Attachment Responses to Their Stockperson." *Journal of Animal Science* 78 (2000) 879–84.

Borowski, Oded. "Animals in the Religions of Syria Palestine." In *A History of the Animal World of the Ancient Near East*, edited by Billie Jean Collins, 405–24. Handbook of Oriental Studies 1.64. Leiden: Brill, 2001.

———. *Every Living Thing: Daily Use of Animals in Ancient Israel*. Walnut Creek, CA: AltaMira, 1998.

Bouissou, M. F. "Influence of Body Weight and Presence of Horns on Social Rank in Domestic Cattle." *Animal Behaviour* 20 (1972) 474–77.

Brooks, P. H., and D. J. A. Cole. "The Effect of the Presence of a Boar on the Attainment of Puberty in Gilts." *Reproduction* 23 (1970) 435–40.

Bunderson, J. Stuart, and Jeffery A. Thompson. "The Call of the Wild: Zookeepers, Callings, and the Double-Edged Sword of Deeply Meaningful Work." *Administrative Science Quarterly* 54 (2009) 32–57.

Bunimovitz, Shlomo, and Avraham Faust. "Building Identity: The Four-Room House and the Israelite Mind." In *Symbiosis, Symbolism, and the Power of the Past: Canaan, Ancient Israel, and Their Neighbours from the Late Bronze Age through Roman Palestina*, edited by William G. Dever and Seymour Gitin, 411–23. Winona Lake, IN: Eisenbrauns, 2003.

Burton, Rob J. F., Sue Peoples, and Mark H. Cooper. "Building 'Cowshed Cultures': A Cultural Perspective on the Promotion of Stockmanship and Animal Welfare on Dairy Farms." *Journal of Rural Studies* 28 (2012) 174–87.

Camerlink, Irene, and Winanda W. Ursinus. "Tail Postures and Tail Motion in Pigs: A Review." *Applied Animal Behaviour Science* 230 (2020) 105079.

Carmichael, Calum M. "On Separating Life and Death: An Explanation of Some Biblical Laws." *Harvard Theological Review* 69 (1976) 1–7.

Chen, Brian L., Kathryn L. Haith, and Breadley A. Mullens. "Beak Condition Drives Abundance and Grooming-Mediated Competitive Asymmetry in a Poultry Ectoparasite Community." *Parasitology* 138 (2011) 748–57.

Chenoweth, P. J. "Libido and Mating Behaviour in Bulls, Boars, and Rams." *Theriogenology* 16 (1981) 155–77.

Collias, Nicholas E., and Elsie C. Collias. "Social Organization of a Red Junglefowl, *Gallus gallus*, Population Related to Evolution Theory." *Animal Behaviour* 51 (1996) 1337–54.

Collias, Nicholas, Elsie Collias, and Robert I. Jennrich. "Dominant Red Junglefowl (*Gallus gallus*) Hens in an Unconfined Flock Rear the Most Young over Their Lifetime." *The Auk* 111 (1994) 863–72.

Bibliography

Collins, Billie Jean. "Animals in the Religions of Ancient Anatolia." In *A History of the Animal World of the Ancient Near East*, edited by Billie Jean Collins, 309–34. Handbook of Oriental Studies 1.64. Leiden: Brill, 2001.

Common Worship: Services and Prayers for the Church of England. London: Church House Publishing, 2000.

Dardaillon, Maryse. "Wild Boar Social Groupings and Their Seasonal Changes in the Camargue, Southern France." *Zeitschrift Säugetierkunde* 53 (1988) 22–30.

Daycard, Laurent. "Structure sociale de la population de bovins sauvages de l'Île Amsterdam, sud de l'Océan Indien." *Revue d'Écologie* 45 (1990) 35–53.

Douglas, Mary. "The Forbidden Animals in Leviticus." *Journal for the Study of the Old Testament* 59 (1993) 3–23.

———. *Purity and Danger: An Analysis of Concepts of Pollution and Taboo.* New ed. London: Routledge, 2002.

Duncan, J. H., and V. G. Kite. "Nest Site Selection and Nest-Building Behaviour in Domestic Fowl." *Animal Behaviour* 37 (1989) 215–31.

Ellingsen, Kristian, Grahame J. Coleman, Vonne Lund, and Cecilie M. Mejdell. "Using Qualitative Behaviour Assessment to Explore the Link between Stockperson Behaviour and Dairy Calf Behaviour." *Applied Animal Behaviour Science* 153 (2014) 10–17.

Epstein, H. *The Awassi Sheep with Special Reference to the Improved Dairy Type.* Rome: Food and Agriculture Organization of the United Nations, 1985.

Fairholme, Edward G., and Wellesley Pain. *A Century of Work for Animals: The History of the R.S.P.C.A., 1824–1924.* London: John Murray, 1924.

Farley, Edward. *Divine Empathy: A Theology of God.* Minneapolis, MN: Fortress, 1996.

Festa-Bianchet, Marco. "Seasonal Dispersion of Overlapping Mountain Sheep Ewe Groups." *Journal of Wildlife Management* 50 (1986) 325–30.

———. "The Social System of Bighorn Sheep: Grouping Patterns, Kinship and Female Dominance Rank." *Animal Behaviour* 42 (1991) 71–82.

Fischer, Gloria J. "The Behaviour of Chickens." In *The Behaviour of Domestic Animals*, edited by E. S. E. Hafez, 454–89. 3rd ed. London: Tindall, 1975.

Fischer, Helga. "Das Triumphgeschrei der Graugans *(Anser anser)*." *Zeitschrift für Tierpsychologie* 22 (1965) 247–304.

Fisher, Andrew, and Lindsay Matthews. "The Social Behaviour of Sheep." In *Social Behaviour in Farm Animals*, edited by L. J. Keeling and H. W. Gonyou, 211–45. Oxford: CABI, 2001.

Fu, Ling-ling, Bo Zhou, Hui-zhi Li, Ting-ting Liang, Qing-po Chu, Allan P. Schinckel, Yuan Li, and Fei-long Xu. "Effects of Tail Docking and/or Teeth Clipping on Behavior, Lesions, and Physiological Indicators of Sows and Their Piglets." *Animal Science Journal* 90 (2019) 1320–32.

Fukasawa, Michiru, Masatoshi Kawahata, Yumi Higashiyama, and Tokushi Komatsu. "Relationship between the Stockperson's Attitudes and Dairy Productivity in Japan." *Animal Science Journal* 88 (2017) 394–400.

Bibliography

Geist, Valerius. "The Evolutionary Significance of Mountain Sheep Horns." *Evolution* 20 (1966) 558–66.

Gentle, M. J., B. O. Hughes, and R. C. Hubrecht. "The Effect of Beak Trimming on Food Intake, Feeding Behaviour and Body Weight in Adult Hens." *Applied Animal Ethology* 8 (1982) 147–59.

Goodridge, John. "The Case of John Dyer's Fat-Tailed Sheep and Their Tail-Trolleys: 'A Thing to Some Scarce Credible.'" *Agricultural History Review* 54 (2006) 229–39.

Gootwine, Elisha. *Physical Appearance of Sheep in Ancient Times in Israel and Its Neighbouring Countries, Mesopotamia and Mediterranean Countries, based on Archaeological Evidence.* Tel Aviv: Agricultural Research Organization, 2017.

Grubb, P. "Social Organization of Soay Sheep and the Behaviour of Ewes and Lambs." In *Island Survivors: The Ecology of the Soay Sheep of St Kilda*, edited by P. A. Jewell, C. Milner, and J. Morton Boyd, 131–59. London: Athlone, 1974.

Grumett, David. "Animals in Christian Theology." *Religion Compass* 5 (2011) 579–88.

———. "Food." In *T. & T. Clark Handbook of the Doctrine of Creation*, edited by Jason Goroncy, 787–98. London: T. & T. Clark, 2024.

———. "Mosaic Food Rules in Celtic Spirituality in Ireland." In *Eating and Believing: Interdisciplinary Perspectives on Vegetarianism and Theology*, edited by Rachel Muers and David Grumett, 31–43. London: T. & T. Clark, 2008.

Grumett, David, and Andrew Butterworth. "Electric Shock Control of Farmed Animals: Welfare Review and Ethical Critique." *Animal Welfare* 31 (2022) 373–85.

Gustafsson, Maria, Per Jensen, Francien H. de Jonge, Gudrun Illmann, and Marek Spinka. "Maternal Behaviour of Domestic Sows and Crosses between Domestic Sows and Wild Boar." *Applied Animal Behaviour Science* 65 (1999) 29–42.

Hafez, E. S. E., and M. F. Bouissou. "The Behaviour of Cattle." In *The Behaviour of Domestic Animals*, edited by E. S. E. Hafez, 203–45. 3rd ed. London: Tindall, 1975.

Hall, Stephen J. G. "Chillingham Cattle: Social and Maintenance Behaviour in an Ungulate That Breeds All Year Round." *Animal Behaviour* 38 (1989) 215–25.

Hall, S. J. G., and G. F. Moore. "Feral Cattle of Swona, Orkney Islands." *Mammal Review* 16 (1986) 89–96.

Hanna, D., I. A. Sneddon, and V. E. Beattie. "The Relationship between the Stockperson's Personality and Attitudes and the Productivity of Dairy Cows." *Animal* 3 (2009) 737–43.

Hansen, L. L., H. Mejer, S. M. Thamsborg, D. V. Byrne, A. Roepstorff, A. H. Karlsson, J. Hansen-Møller, M. T. Jensen, and M. Tuomola. "Influence of

Bibliography

Chicory Roots (*Cichorium intybus* L) on Boar Taint in Entire Male and Female Pigs." *Animal Science* 82 (2006) 359–68.

Hansen, Lars P., Nina Jonsson, and Bror Jonsson. "Oceanic Migration in Homing Atlantic Salmon." *Animal Behaviour* 45 (1993) 927–41.

Hartley, Dorothy. *Food in England*. London: Macdonald, 1954.

Hass, Christine C., and Donald A. Jenni. "Social Play among Juvenile Bighorn Sheep: Structure, Development, and Relationship to Adult Behavior." *Ethology* 93 (1993) 105–16.

Haulenbeek, Andrea M., and Larry S. Katz. "Female Tail Wagging Enhances Sexual Performance in Male Goats." *Hormones and Behavior* 60 (2011) 244–47.

Hemsworth, Paul H., and Grahame J. Coleman. *Human–Livestock Interactions: The Stockperson and the Productivity and Welfare of Intensively Farmed Animals*. 2nd ed. Wallingford: CABI, 2011.

Hernández, Joaquín, José Luis Benedito, Angel Abuelo, and Cristina Castillo. "Ruminal Acidosis in Feedlot: From Aetiology to Prevention." *Scientific World Journal* (2014) 702575.

Hinch, G. N., J. J. Lynch, and C. J. Thwaites. "Patterns and Frequency of Social Interactions in Young Grazing Bulls and Steers." *Applied Animal Ethology* 9 (1982) 15–30.

Hiuser, Kris, and Matthew Barton. "A Promise Is a Promise: God's Covenantal Relationship with Animals." *Scottish Journal of Theology* 67 (2014) 340–56.

Hoefs, M. "The Thermoregulatory Potential of *Ovis* Horn Cores." *Canadian Journal of Zoology* 78 (2000) 1419–26.

Hoffman, Jessica M., and Teresa G. Valencak. "A Short Life on the Farm: Aging and Longevity in Agricultural, Large-Bodied Mammals." *GeroScience* 42 (2020) 909–22.

Horrell, R. I., P. J. A'Ness, S. A. Edwards, and J. C. Eddison. "The Use of Nose-Rings in Pigs: Consequences for Rooting, Other Functional Activities, and Welfare." *Animal Welfare* 10 (2001) 3–22.

Hughes, B. O., I. J. H. Duncan, and Margretta F. Brown. "The Performance of Nest Building by Domestic Hens: Is It More Important Than the Construction of a Nest?" *Animal Behaviour* 37 (1989) 210–14.

Hughes, P. E., G. P. Pearce, and A. M. Paterson. "Mechanisms Mediating the Stimulatory Effects of the Boar on Gilt Reproduction." *Journal of Reproduction and Fertility Supplement* 40 (1990) 323–41.

Hurnik, J. F. "Sexual Behavior of Female Domestic Mammals." *Veterinary Clinics of North America: Food Animal Practice* 3 (1987) 423–61.

Ishiwata, Toshie, Katsuji Uetake, Robert J. Kilgour, Yusuke Eguchi, and Toshio Tanaka. "Comparison of Time Budget of Behaviors between Penned and Ranged Young Cattle Focused on General and Oral Behaviors." *Animal Science Journal* 79 (2008) 518–25.

Javed, Sálim, and Asad R. Rahmani. "Flocking and Habitat Use Pattern of the Red Junglefowl *Gallus gallus* in Dudwa National Park, India." *Tropical Ecology* 41 (2000) 11–16.

Bibliography

Jensen, Per. "Observations on the Maternal Behaviour of Free-Ranging Domestic Pigs." *Applied Animal Behaviour Science* 16 (1986) 131–42.

Jeremias, Joachim. *Jerusalem in the Time of Jesus: An Investigation into Economic and Social Conditions during the New Testament Period.* Translated by F. H. Cave and C. H. Cave. London: SCM, 1969.

Jezierski, Włodzimierz. "Longevity and Morality Rate in a Population of Wild Boar." *Acta Theriologica* 22 (1977) 337–48.

Jones, Gillian G., and Peta Sadler. "A Review of Published Sources for Age at Death in Cattle." *Environmental Archaeology* 17 (2012) 1–10.

Jonsson, Bror, Jan Henning L'Abée-Lund, Tor G. Heggberget, Arne J. Jensen, Bjrn O. Johnsen, Tor F. Næsje, and Leif M. Sættem. "Longevity, Body Size, and Growth in Anadromous Brown Trout (*Salmo trutta*)." *Canadian Journal of Fisheries and Aquatic Sciences* 48 (1991) 1838–45.

Josephus. *The Jewish War.* Vol. 2. Translated by H. St. J. Thackeray. Cambridge: Harvard University Press, 1928.

Kallio-Nyberg, I., and E. Ikonen. "Migration Pattern of Two Salmon Stocks in the Baltic Sea." *ICES Journal of Marine Science* 49 (1992) 191–98.

Kaukonen, Eija, and Anna Valros. "Feather Pecking and Cannibalism in Non-Beak-Trimmed Laying Hen Flocks—Farmers' Perspectives." *Animals* 9 (2019) 43.

Keel, Othmar. *Das Böcklein in der Milch seiner Mutter und Verwandtes : im Lichte eines altorientalischen Bildmotivs.* Göttingen: Vandenhoeck & Ruprecht, 1980.

Kendrick, Keith M., Khia Atkins, Michael R. Hinton, Kevin D. Broad, C. Fabre-Nys, and Barry Keverne. "Facial and Vocal Discrimination in Sheep." *Animal Behaviour* 49 (1995) 1665–76.

Kenyon, P. R., C. Viñoles, and S. T. Morris. "Effect of Teasing by the Ram on the Onset of Puberty in Romney Ewe Lambs." *New Zealand Journal of Agricultural Research* 55 (2012) 283–91.

Kheravii, S. K., N. K. Morgan, R. A. Swick, M. Choct, and S.-B. Wu. "Roles of Dietary Fibre and Ingredient Particle Size in Broiler Nutrition." *World's Poultry Science Journal* 74 (2018) 301–16.

Kiley, M. "A Review of the Advantages and Disadvantages of Castrating Farm Livestock with Particular Reference to Behavioural Effects." *British Veterinary Journal* 132 (1976) 323–31.

Kiley-Worthington, M. "Tail Movements of Ungulates, Canids and Felids with Particular Reference to Their Causation and Function as Displays." *Behaviour* 56 (1976) 69–114.

Klemm, W. R., C. J. Sherry, L. M. Schake, and R. F. Sis. "Homosexual Behavior in Feedlot Steers: An Aggression Hypothesis." *Applied Animal Ethology* 11 (1983/84) 187–95.

Knierim, Ute, Nora Irrgang, and Beatrice A. Roth. "To Be or Not to Be Horned—Consequences in Cattle." *Livestock Science* 179 (2015) 29–37.

Kotrschal, Kurt, Josef Hemetsberger, and Brigitte M. Weiss. "Making the Best of a Bad Situation: Homosociality in Male Greylag Geese." In *Homosexual*

Bibliography

Behaviour in Animals: An Evolutionary Perspective, edited by Volker Sommer and Paul L. Vasey, 45–76. Cambridge University Press, 2006.

Krohn, C. C., X. Boivin, and J. G. Jago. "The Presence of the Dam during Handling Prevents the Socialization of Young Calves to Humans." *Applied Animal Behaviour Science* 80 (2003) 263–75.

Krohn, C. C., J. G. Jago, and X. Boivin. "The Effect of Early Handling on the Socialisation of Young Calves to Humans." *Applied Animal Behaviour Science* 74 (2001) 121–33.

Lambert, W. G. *Ancient Mesopotamian Religion and Mythology.* Edited by A. R. George and T. M. Oshima. Orientalische Religionen in der Antike 15. Tübingen: Mohr Siebeck, 2016.

Larrère, Catherine, and Raphael Larrère. "Animal Rearing as a Contract?" *Journal of Agricultural and Environmental Ethics* 12 (2000) 51–58.

Lawrence, A. B. "Mother, Daughter and Peer Relationships of Scottish Hill Sheep." *Animal Behaviour* 39 (1990) 481–87.

Lazo, Alfonso. "Social Segregation and the Maintenance of Social Stability in a Feral Cattle Population." *Animal Behaviour* 48 (1994) 1133–41.

Leeuw, J. A. de, J. E. Bolhuis, G. Bosch, and W. J. J. Gerrits. "Effects of Dietary Fibre on Behaviour and Satiety in Pigs." *Proceedings of the Nutrition Society* 67 (2008) 334–42.

Levin, Schneir. "Albinism and Genetics in the Bible." *Jewish Bible Quarterly* 31 (2003) 57–59.

Lincoln, Lucy. "Translating Hebrew and Greek Terms for Sheep and Goats." *Bible Translator* 47 (1996) 322–35.

Livy. *History of Rome.* Vol. 3. Translated by J. C. Yardley. Loeb Classical Library 172. Cambridge: Harvard University Press, 1924.

Lott, Dale F., and Benjamin L. Hart. "Applied Ethology in a Nomadic Cattle Culture." *Applied Animal Ethology* 5 (1979) 309–19.

Lubac, Henri de. *Catholicism: Christ and the Common Destiny of Man.* Translated by Lancelot C. Sheppard and Elizabeth Englund. San Francisco: Ignatius, 1988.

Luther, Martin. *Works.* 55 vols. St. Louis, MO: Concordia, 1955–86.

MacDonald, Nathan. *What Did the Ancient Israelites Eat? Diet in Biblical Times.* Grand Rapids: Eerdmans, 2008.

Martin, G. B., J. T. B. Milton, R. H. Davidson, G. E. Banchero Hunzicker, D. R. Lindsay, and D. Blache. "Natural Methods for Increasing Reproductive Efficiency in Small Ruminants." *Animal Reproduction Science* 82–83 (2004) 231–46.

Martin, Jessica E., Sarah H. Ison, and Emma M. Baxter. "The Influence of Neonatal Environment on Piglet Play Behaviour and Post-Weaning Social and Cognitive Development." *Applied Animal Behaviour Science* 163 (2015) 69–79.

Mintline, Erin M., Sara L. Wood, Anne Mariede Passillé, Jeffrey Rushen, and Cassandra B. Tucker. "Assessing Calf Play Behavior in an Arena Test." *Applied Animal Behaviour Science* 141 (2012) 101–7.

Bibliography

Monje, A. R., R. Alberio, G. Schiersmann, J. Chedrese, N. Caroú, and S. S. Callejas. "Male Effect on the Post-Partum Sexual Activity of Cows Maintained on Two Nutritional Levels." *Animal Reproduction Science* 29 (1992) 145–56.

Murray, Robert. *The Cosmic Covenant: Biblical Themes of Justice, Peace, and the Integrity of Creation.* London: Sheed & Ward, 1992.

Newberry, R. C., and D. G. M. Wood-Gush. "Development of Some Behaviour Patterns in Piglets under Semi-Natural Conditions." *Animal Production* 46 (1988) 103–9.

———. "Social Relationships of Piglets in a Semi-Natural Environment." *Animal Behaviour* 34 (1986) 1311–18.

Oliveira, Daiana de, Mateus J. R. Paranhos da Costa, Manja Zupan, Therese Rehn, and Linda J. Keeling. "Early Human Handling in Non-Weaned Piglets: Effects on Behaviour and Body Weight." *Applied Animal Behaviour Science* 164 (2015) 56–63.

Olsson, I. Anna S., and Linda J. Keeling. "Why in Earth? Dustbathing Behaviour in Jungle and Domestic Fowl Reviewed from a Tinbergian and Animal Welfare Perspective." *Applied Animal Behaviour Science* 93 (2005) 259–82.

Origen. *Homilies on Leviticus, 1–16.* Translated by Gary Wayne Barkley. Fathers of the Church 83. Washington, DC: Catholic University of America Press, 1990.

Parés-Casanova, Pere M., and Marta Caballero. "Possible Tendency of Polled Cattle towards Larger Ears." *Revista Colombiana de Ciencias Pecurias* 27 (2014) 221–25.

Park, Song-Mi Suzie. "Transformation and Demarcation of Jacob's 'Flocks' in Genesis 30:25–43: Identity, Election, and the Role of the Divine." *Catholic Biblical Quarterly* 72 (2010) 667–77.

Pauly, C., P. Spring, J. V. O'Doherty, S. Ampuero Kragten, and G. Bee. "Performances, Meat Quality and Boar Taint of Castrates and Entire Male Pigs Fed a Standard and a Raw Potato Starch-Enriched Diet." *Animal* 2 (2008) 1707–15.

Pearson, J. D. "A Mendelian Interpretation of Jacob's Sheep." *Science and Christian Belief* 13 (2001) 51–58.

Pelletier, Fanie, Julien Mainguy, and Steeve D. Côté. "Rut-Induced Hypophagia in Male Bighorn Sheep and Mountain Goats: Foraging under Time Budget Constraints." *Ethology* 115 (2009) 141–51.

Petersen, H. V., K. Vestergaard, and P. Jensen. "Integration of Piglets into Social Groups of Free-Ranging Domestic Pigs." *Applied Animal Behaviour Science* 23 (1989) 223–36.

Philo. *On the Special Laws.* Vol. 1. Translated by F. H. Colson. Loeb Classical Library 320. Cambridge: Harvard University Press, 1937.

Physiologus: A Medieval Book of Nature Law. Translated by Michael J. Curley. Chicago: University of Chicago Press, 2009.

Plessis, I. du, C. van der Waal, and E. C. Webb. "A Comparison of Plant Form and Browsing Height Selection of Four Small Stock Breeds—Preliminary

Bibliography

Results." *South African Journal of Animal Science* 34 (2004) supplement 1, 31–34.

Porcher, Jocelyne. "The Relationship between Workers and Animals in the Pork Industry: A Shared Suffering." *Journal of Agricultural and Environmental Ethics* 24 (2011) 3–17.

Porcher, Jocelyne, and Tiphaine Schmitt. "Dairy Cows: Workers in the Shadows?" *Society & Animals* 20 (2012) 39–60.

Probst, Johanna K., Edna Hillmann, Florian Leiber, Michael Kreuzer, and Anet Spengler Neff. "Influence of Gentle Touching Applied Few Weeks before Slaughter on Avoidance Distance and Slaughter Stress in Finishing Cattle." *Applied Animal Behaviour Science* 144 (2013) 14–21.

Probst, Johanna K., Anet Spengler Neff, Florian Leiber, Michael Kreuzer, and Edna Hillmann. "Gentle Touching in Early Life Reduces Avoidance Distance and Slaughter Stress in Beef Cattle." *Applied Animal Behaviour Science* 139 (2012) 42–49.

Reinhardt, Catherine, Annie Reinhardt, and Viktor Reinhardt. "Social Behaviour and Reproductive Performance in Semi-Wild Scottish Highland Cattle." *Applied Animal Behaviour Science* 15 (1986) 125–36.

Rekwot, Peter, David Ogwu, Emmanuel Oyedipe, and Victor Sekoni. "Effects of Bull Exposure and Body Growth on Onset of Puberty in Bunaji and Friesian X Bunaji Heifers." *Reproduction Nutrition Development* 40 (2000) 359–67.

———. "The Role of Pheromones and Biostimulation in Animal Reproduction." *Animal Reproduction Science* 65 (2001) 157–70.

Riber, Anja Brinch, Anette Wichman, Bjarne O. Braastad, and Björn Forkman. "Effects of Broody Hens on Perch Use, Ground Pecking, Feather Pecking and Cannibalism in Domestic Fowl (*Gallus gallus domesticus*)." *Applied Animal Behaviour Science* 106 (2007) 39–51.

Rodríguez-Estévez, V., A. García, F. Peña, and A. G. Gómez. "Foraging of Iberian Fattening Pigs Grazing Natural Pasture in the Dehesa." *Livestock Science* 120 (2009) 135–43.

Roselli, C. H. E., C. R. Radhika, and K. R. Kaufman. "The Development of Male-Oriented Behavior in Rams." *Frontiers in Neuroendocrinology* 32 (2011) 164–69.

Sambraus, Hans Hinrich, and Dörte Sambraus. "Prägung von Nutzieren auf Menschen." *Zeitschrift für Tierpsychologie* 38 (1975) 1–17.

Sandom, Christopher J., Joelene Hughes, and David W. Macdonald. "Rewilding the Scottish Highlands: Do Wild Boar, *Sus scrofa*, Use a Suitable Foraging Strategy to Be Effective Ecosystem Engineers?" *Restoration Ecology* 21 (2013) 336–43.

Sapir-Hen, Lidar, Guy Bar-Oz, Yuval Gadot, and Israel Finkelstein. "Pig Husbandry in Iron Age Israel and Judah: New Insights Regarding the Origin of the 'Taboo.'" *Zeitschrift des Deutschen Palästina-Vereins* 129 (2013) 1–20.

Bibliography

Scholtz, Ansie and Schalk Cloete. "The Lamb's Tail: Production." *Red Meat/ Rooivleis* 7 (2016) 66–69.

Scurlock, JoAnn. "Animals in Ancient Mesopotamian Religion." In *A History of the Animal World of the Ancient Near East*, edited by Billie Jean Collins, 361–87. Handbook of Oriental Studies 1.64. Leiden: Brill, 2001.

Segerdahl, Pär. "Can Natural Behaviour Be Cultivated? The Farm as a Local Human/Animal Culture." *Journal of Agricultural and Environmental Ethics* 20 (2007) 167–93.

Shackleton, D. M., and C. C. Shank. "A Review of the Social Behavior of Feral and Wild Sheep and Goats." *Journal of Animal Science* 58 (1984) 500–509.

Sibbald, Angela M., Hans W. Erhard, James E. McLeod, and Russell J. Hooper. "Individual Personality and the Spatial Distribution of Groups of Grazing Animals: An Example with Sheep." *Behavioural Processes* 82 (2009) 319–26.

Signoret, J. P., B. A. Baldwin, D. Fraser, and E. S. E. Hafez. "The Behaviour of Swine." In *The Behaviour of Domestic Animals*, edited by E. S. E. Hafez, 295–329. 3rd ed. London: Tindall, 1975.

Stafford, K. J., and N. G. Gregory. "Implications of Intensification of Pastoral Animal Production on Animal Welfare." *New Zealand Veterinary Journal* 56 (2008) 274–80.

Stephens, D. B., and J. L. Linzell. "The Development of Sucking Behaviour in the Newborn Goat." *Animal Behaviour* 22 (1974) 628–33.

Stolba, A., and D. G. M. Wood-Gush. "The Behaviour of Pigs in a Semi-Natural Environment." *Animal Production* 48 (1989) 419–25.

Stricklin, W. R. "Evolution and Domestication of Social Behaviour." In *Social Behaviour in Farm Animals*, edited by L. J. Keeling and H. W. Gonyou, 83–110. Wallingford: CABI, 2001.

Tallet, Céline, Sophie Brajon, Nicolas Devillers, and Joop Lensink. "Pig-Human Interactions: Creating a Positive Perception of Humans to Ensure Pig Welfare." In *Advances in Pig Welfare*, edited by Marek Špinka, 381–98. Cambridge: Woodhead, 2017.

Taylor, Charles R. "The Vascularity and Possible Thermoregulatory Function of the Horns in Goats." *Physiological Zoology* 39 (1966) 127–39.

Teeter, Emily. "Animals in Egyptian Religion." In *A History of the Animal World of the Ancient Near East*, edited by Billie Jean Collins, 335–60. Handbook of Oriental Studies 1.64. Leiden: Brill, 2001.

Thogmartin, Wayne E. "Home-Range Size and Habitat Selection of Female Wild Turkeys (*Meleagris gallopavo*) in Arkansas." *American Midland Naturalist* 145 (2001) 247–60.

Thorpe, John E. "Salmon Migration." *Science Progress* 72 (1988) 345–70.

Thorstad, Eva B., Christopher D. Todd, Ingebrigt Uglem, Pål Arne Bjørn, Patrick G. Gargan, Knut Wiik Vollset, Elina Halttunen, Steinar Kålås, Marius Berg, and Bengt Finstad. "Marine Life of the Sea Trout." *Marine Biology* 163 (2016) 47.

Bibliography

Tong, Q., C. E. Romanini, V. Exadaktylos, C. Bahr, D. Berckmans, H. Bergoug, N. Eterradossi, N. Roulston, R. Verhelst, I. M. McGonnell, and T. Demmers. "Embryonic Development and the Physiological Factors That Coordinate Hatching in Domestic Chickens." *Poultry Science* 92 (2013) 620–28.

Tornero, Carlos, Marie Balasse, Stéphanie Bréhard, Isabelle Carrère, Denis Fiorillo, Jean Guilaine, Jean-Denis Vigne, and Claire Manen. "Early Evidence of Sheep Lambing De-Seasoning in the Western Mediterranean in the Sixth Millennium BCE." *Nature Scientific Reports* 10 (2020) 12798.

Ulishney, Megan Loumagne. "The Evolution of *Homo Ludens*: Sexual Selection and a Theology of Play." *Zygon* 57 (2022) 564–75.

Ungerfeld, R., L. Lacuesta, J. P. Damián, and J. Giriboni. "Does Heterosexual Experience Matter for Bucks' Homosexual Mating Behavior?" *Journal of Veterinary Behavior* 8 (2013) 471–74.

Ungerfeld, R., M. A. Ramos, and A. Bielli. "Relationship between Male–Male and Male–Female Sexual Behavior in 5–6-Month-Old Male Lambs." *Animal Reproduction Science* 100 (2007) 385–90.

Valníčková, B., I. Stěhulová, R. Šárová, and M. Špinka. "The Effect of Age at Separation from the Dam and Presence of Social Companions on Play Behavior and Weight Gain in Dairy Calves." *Journal of Dairy Science* 98 (2015) 5545–56.

VanDrunen, David. *Divine Covenants and Moral Order: A Biblical Theology of Natural Law.* Grand Rapids: Eerdmans, 2014.

Veissier, Isabelle, D. Lamy, and P. Le Neindre. "Social Behaviour in Domestic Beef Cattle When Yearling Calves Are Left with the Cows for the Next Calving." *Applied Animal Behaviour Science* 27 (1990) 193–200.

Ventorp, M., and P. Michanek. "Cow–Calf Behaviour in Relation to First Suckling." *Research in Veterinary Science* 51 (1991) 6–10.

Vince, Margaret A. "Response of the Newly Born Clun Forest Lamb to Maternal Vocalisations." *Behaviour* 96 (1986) 164–70.

Waiblinger, Susanne, and Christoph Menke. "Influence of Herd Size on Human–Cow Relationships." *Anthrozoös* 12 (1999) 240–47.

White, Nicholas R. "Effects of Embryonic Auditory Stimulation on Hatch Time in the Domestic Chick." *Bird Behavior* 5 (1984) 122–26.

Whitehead, G. Kenneth. *The Ancient White Cattle of Britain and Their Descendants.* London: Faber and Faber, 1953.

Williams, J. L., S. J. G. Hall, M. Del Corvo, K. T. Ballingall, L. Colli, P. Ajmone Marsan, and F. Biscarini. "Inbreeding and Purging at the Genomic Level: The Chillingham Cattle Reveal Extensive, Non-Random SNP Heterozygosity." *Animal Genetics* 47 (2015) 19–27.

Wiltschko, Wolfgang, Rafael Freire, Ursula Munro, Thorsten Ritz, Lesley Rogers, Peter Thalau, and Roswitha Wiltschko. "The Magnetic Compass of Domestic Chickens, *Gallus gallus*." *Journal of Experimental Biology* 210 (2007) 2300–2310.

Bibliography

Wischner, Diane, Nicole Kemper, and Joachim Krieter. "Nest-Building Behaviour in Sows and Consequences for Pig Husbandry." *Livestock Science* 124 (2009) 1–8.

Workman, Lance, and Richard John Andrew. "Simultaneous Changes in Behaviour and in Lateralization during the Development of Male and Female Domestic Chicks." *Animal Behaviour* 38 (1989) 596–605.

Scriptural Index

Genesis

1:9–13	54, 57
1:24–26	72
1:26	69, 70
1:27	70
1:28	69
1:30	57
2:10–14	54
5:1	70
6:11—8:19	75
6:18	75
7:2a	9
8:11	61
9:2–3	54
9:4–5	9
9:6	70
9:10	75
12:16	9
13:5	9
15:9	48
18:7	9
20:14	9
21:27	9
22:13	48
24:19–20	78
24:25	78
25:21–26	46
27:11–23	84
29:4–10	77
30:32—31:12	46
30:32	9
31:38	48
32:13–14	46
36:7	46
37:13	59
37:16	59

Exodus

2:16–19	77
9:3	2
12:5	31
12:21–27	33
22:30	26
23:19b	26
29:1	31
29:22	38
34:26	26

Leviticus

1:3, 10	31
3:1, 6	31
3:9	38
4:3	31
4:23	31
4:28	31
4:32	31
5:15	31
5:18	31
6:6	31
7:3	38
8:25	38

Leviticus (continued)

9:19	38
11:3–6	59
11:3	54
11:9	54
14:10	31
22:19	32
22:22	33
22:24–25	33
22:27	26
22:28	26
25:43	71
25:46	71
25:53	71

Numbers

6:14	32
19:2	32
28:3	32
28:9	32
28:19	32
28:27	32
28:31	32
28:11	48
29:2	32
29:8	32
29:13	32
29:17	32
29:20	32
29:23	32
29:26	32
29:29	32
29:32	32
29:35	32
35:2–7	59

Deuteronomy

14:6	54, 59
14:21	26
17:1	32
25:4	60
32:14	48

Joshua

14:4	59
21:1–42	59

1 Samuel

9:24	47
15:9	48
28:24	57

2 Samuel

5:2	78
12:1–4	9

1 Kings

4:24	71
7:25	70

1 Chronicles

4:39–40	59
27:29	59

2 Chronicles

8:10	71

Job

12:7	23
39:1–3	23
39:14–15	25
40:20	64

Psalms

1:2	59
8:7–8	54, 62
29:1	11
29:6	64
68:27	71
72:8	71
80:3	24

Scriptural Index

84:3	25	43:22–25	32
104:17	25	45:18	32
114:4	64	45:23	32
114:6	64	45:25	32
148:7–10	66	46:4	33
150:6	66	46:6	33

Proverbs
11:22	43

Amos
6:4	48, 58

Ecclesiastes
3:2	62

Habakkuk
3:17	58

Song of Songs
2:9	17
2:17	17
2:12	61
4:2	25
6:5	9
8:14	17

Malachi
4:2	58

Prayer of Azariah
57–59	66

Isaiah
16:1	48
34:15	25

2 Esdras
1:30	27

Jeremiah
8:7	61
46:21	57
48:28	25

Matthew
1:25	78
2:6b	78
2:11	1
6:26	54
8:20	25
8:30–32	9, 42
10:5–6	10
12:11	9
21:28–32	17
23:37	27, 85
24:32–33	78
25:32–34	9, 10
26:34	16
26:74b	16

Ezekiel
4:2	40
21:22	40
27:21	48
34:3	2
34:5	2
34:8	2
34:17	9
38:20	54

Mark

5:11–13	9, 42
13:28–29	78
14:30	16
14:72	16

Luke

1:34	78
2:6	1
2:8	9
8:10	78
8:17	78
8:32–33	9, 42
13:34	27, 85
18:34	78
21:30–31	78
22:34	16
22:60–62	16
24:35	78

John

2:25	78

6:15	78
8:32	78
10:14	77
10:16	13
10:27	74, 77
12:16	78
13:38	16
14:17	78
18:27	16
16:19	78
21:15–17	10, 78, 85

1 Timothy

5:18a	60

Hebrews

13:20	10

2 Peter

2:22	54

Subject Index

Aaron, 31
Abraham, 9, 47–48
acorn, 43
Aegean Sea, 62
age, 6, 15, 23, 50; see also lifespan
altricial, 2, 52
Amalekites, 48
Ambrose of Milan, 12, 21, 62
Amos, 48, 57–58
Amsterdam Island, 14
androstenone, 36
anthropocentrism, 2
apostle, 85
ark, 9, 75
ascent, 59
assertiveness, 15
assurance scheme, 68, 91
attitude, 76–77, 80–81
Augustine of Hippo, 7–9, 26
automation, 87–88
Awassi sheep, 37, 47

Baal, 70
Baltic Sea, 63
baptism, 26
Basil of Caesarea, 10–11, 12, 40,
    62
battering ram, 40
behavior, 18, 21–22, 25, 28, 34–36,
    50, 52–67
Behemoth, 64
Benjamin, 71
bestiary, 8

Bethlehem, 78
birth, 2, 4, 18, 23–26, 42, 50,
    52–53, 62, 69, 72, 82–84
bishop, 8, 10, 12, 26, 29, 40, 62
Black Sea, 62
blemish, 31–33
blood, 3, 33, 36, 41
boar, 17, 19, 24, 35–36, 49, 60
"boar taint," 36
branch, 24
breeding, 14–15, 34–35, 43,
    45–47, 48, 49–50, 55, 84,
    85, 88
brown trout, 49, 62–63
browsing, 55, 56, 57
building, 68, 72, 75, 80
bull, 14–15, 18, 31–35, 65, 69,
    70, 81
"buller" syndrome, 20
butting, 28, 64–65

calf, 26, 28, 40, 41, 53, 57–58, 64,
    65, 77, 82, 83–84, 85
camel, 37
carnivore, 52
castration, 33, 35–37, 42, 87
cattle, 8, 9, 14–15, 22, 23, 38,
    40–41, 49–50, 57–58, 86–88;
    see also bull, calf, cow, heifer,
    ox
chewing, 58–59
chick, 16, 27–28, 49, 53, 85

chicken, 2, 16, 44–45, 47, 49, 56, 58, 61, 66–67, 69, 86; *see also* chick, cockerel, hen
chicory, 36
Chillingham herd, 14–15
church, 7, 11, 26, 29, 85
claw, 58–59
cleaning, 86
cockerel, 16, 19
colostrum, 26, 81
comfort, 38–39, 72
community, 7, 73–75, 85
concentrate, 58, 60
consumer, 91
contract, 74–75
courtship, 21
covenant, 75
cow, 14–15, 18–19, 20, 23–24, 28, 34–35, 70, 74, 76, 79, 84, 85, 86–87
cow track, 80
creation, 53–54, 69–70
crops, 81
cud, 58–59

data, 87–88
David, 9, 11, 78
deer, 23; *see also* stag
digestion, 2–3, 4, 58–59
disbudding, 72
disease, 2, 38, 45, 49, 50, 68, 72, 88
dominion, 69–71
dove, 44
dustbathing, 56
duty of care, 68, 75

ear, 41, 63
earthquake, 64
Easter, 10
Eden, 54
egg, 2, 6, 16, 24, 25
Egypt, 33, 57, 70, 77
election, 90
electric shock, 86–87
embryo, 2, 24, 34
empathy, 76–78

Esau, 46, 84
ewe, 11–13, 18–19, 25–26, 35, 37, 38, 39, 46, 48, 65, 69, 73, 85
Ezekiel, 9, 32
Ezra, 27

face, 64, 74
fear, 72, 77, 82, 87
feather, 45, 56
feed, 36, 43, 60–61, 77–78, 86, 87, 88
feeding, 9, 12, 20, 27, 36–37, 40, 43, 44–45, 56–61, 63, 66, 72, 81–89; *see also* browsing, grazing
female, 4, 6, 14–15, 18–19, 20–29, 31, 34, 36–37, 40, 84; *see also* cow, ewe, sow
fencing, 35–37, 46, 82–83, 87
feral, 6–7, 10, 23, 26; *see also* Amsterdam Island, St Kilda, Swona
fertility, 15, 18, 34–35
fibre, 45, 58, 59
fighting, 16, 27, 36, 40, 42–43, 49, 58, 81
First Jewish War, 33
fish, 4, 8, 50, 54, 61–64, 66; *see also* brown trout, salmon
Flavius, 33
fleece, 48
Flood, the, 44, 54, 61, 75
food, 1–2, 23, 27, 37, 38, 40, 42, 49, 54, 56, 57, 59, 62, 66, 68, 71, 73; *see also* feed
forage, 10, 15, 23, 27, 43, 45, 55, 56, 60–61
forest, 24, 43, 55, 56, 61
France, 85

genetics, 15, 34, 39, 43, 48, 49, 73
gizzard, 58
goad, 81
goat, 9, 19, 23, 26–27, 31, 32, 38, 40, 45–46, 47, 53, 56–57, 59, 60, 69, 79; *see also* kid

goose, 2–3, 20–22, 69, 70; see also
    gosling
gosling, 21
grazing, 6, 9, 10, 13, 14, 28, 43, 55,
    56, 59–61, 66, 87
grooming, 4, 17, 40, 45, 60, 65
group, 6–29, 34–37, 45, 47, 50, 58,
    72–73, 81
guilt, 31, 38

habitat, 8, 24, 50, 53–57, 66, 71, 90
handling, 35, 72, 76–77, 82–83
harvest, 32
hatching, 20–21, 24
hawk, 27
heifer, 32, 34, 40, 47
hen, 16, 19, 24, 25, 27–28, 49, 53,
    74, 85
Herod, 78
hierarchy, 11, 13–16, 18, 20, 29,
    40, 65, 73
Hittite, 69, 70
Holy Spirit, 11
hoof, 54–55, 58
horn, 4, 11, 15, 40–41, 48, 64
human, 1–8, 10, 17, 45, 50, 53,
    66, 68–89, 90, 92; see also
    woman

image, 70
indoors, 1, 45, 54, 57, 68, 86,
    87–88
injection, 87
injury, 20, 25, 33, 68, 72, 74, 80, 88
Ireland, 42, 76
Isaac, 48, 77, 84–85
isolation, 35, 81
Israel, 7, 9, 33, 37, 42, 54, 73, 78,
    85
Israelites, 10, 17, 26–27, 30–33,
    48, 69, 71, 75
Italy, 39
Jacob, 45–46, 48, 71, 77, 79, 84–85
Jeroboam, 70
Jerusalem, 27, 32, 33–34, 39, 41,
    70, 85

Jesus, 1, 9–10, 13, 16, 27, 42, 73,
    77, 78, 85
Jethro, 77
Judah, 41
judgment, 9, 61
Juno, 21

kid, 26–27, 81, 84–85
kingdom, 10

Laban, 9, 45–46, 48, 77, 79
lamb, 9, 10, 12–13, 19, 26, 31–34,
    38–39, 45–46, 48, 53, 64–65,
    69, 72, 81–84, 85
lambing, 19, 25–26, 85, 88
lameness, 80, 88
landmark, 54, 61
Last Supper, 33
laying, 20, 74
learning, 6, 11, 50
leg, 47, 56
legislation, 90
leper, 31
licking, 60, 81, 83
lifespan, 47–50
light, 45, 53, 61, 63, 68, 70–71
likeness, 70
Livy, 21
locomotion, 38, 47
longhouse, 73
Luther, Martin, 27, 79
luxury, 58

magnetism, 61, 63
Marmara, Sea of, 62
Mary, 79
maternal bond/care, 12–14,
    25–28, 82–85
mating, 11, 15, 18, 26, 29, 34, 36,
    46
medication, 49, 72, 87
Mesopotamia, 69, 71
migration, 10–11, 20, 38, 61–64
milk, 6, 9, 12, 26, 42–43, 48, 73,
    76, 79, 81, 87, 88
milking, 73, 74, 79, 80, 86

monogamy, 20, 22
moon, 33
Moses, 26, 48, 77
moulting, 20–21
mountain, 9, 10, 17, 23, 41, 48,
    60, 64
mutilation, 30–45, 50–51, 87
mutton, 48–49

Nathan, 9
Nazirite, 32
Neolithic, 85
nest, 20, 27
nesting, 24–25, 54–56
Noah, 9, 44, 54, 61, 75
Norway, 49
nose, 17, 42
novelty, 65
nutrition, 26, 49, 59, 60

oestrus, 18–19, 20, 24
offering, 31–33, 46; see also
    sacrifice
Origen, 59
ostrich, 25
outdoor, 1, 4, 42, 54–55, 68, 75,
    87–88
ox, 32, 59–60

packaging, 91
Palestine, 37
Passover, 31–34
pecking, 25, 28, 44–45
pecking order, 16
perching, 28, 53
personality, 76, 80
pet, 49
Peter, 10, 16, 85
Philistine, 57
Philo, 33
pig, 2, 9, 17, 24–25, 35–36, 38–39,
    41–44, 55, 58, 69, 70, 84, 86;
    see also boar, piglet, sow
piglet, 4, 17, 25, 28, 35, 39, 42–43,
    65–66, 81, 84
play, 28, 39, 60, 64–66, 81

plumage, 56, 66
posture, 10, 38
potato, 36
precocial, 52
predation, 2, 10, 20, 23, 24, 27, 37,
    55, 58–59, 61, 64, 81
preening, 45
prince, 48
priest, 31, 33, 77, 78
productivity, 76, 87
prudence, 78

quick-response code, 91

Rachel, 73, 77
ram, 11, 13–14, 18–19, 31–33,
    35, 38, 40–41, 46–48, 60, 64,
    70, 85
Rebecca, 73, 77–78, 84
reproduction, 16, 18, 33–34, 40
retailer, 91
river, 49, 54, 62–63
robot, 86–87
rodent, 52
Roman, 16, 21, 33
Roman Catholic, 7
rooting, 30, 39, 43–44, 60
Rosh Hashanah, 32
ruler, 31, 32, 48, 78
rumen, 58, 59
rumination, 59, 60

sabbath, 9, 32
sacrifice, 26–27, 30–34, 37–38,
    39, 47–48, 71, 80; see also
    offering
St Kilda, 13
salinity, 62–63
salmon, 63
salvation, 7
Samuel, 47
Saul, 47, 48, 57
sea, 53–54, 61–63
sexual interaction, 17–23, 29, 81
shade, 54

Subject Index

sheep, 9, 10–14, 31, 32, 38, 41,
45–49, 56–57, 74, 77, 85, 88;
see also Awassi sheep, ewe,
lamb, ram
shelter, 26, 54, 68, 73, 92
shepherd, 2, 6, 9, 11, 37, 47,
73–74, 78, 89
sign, 7–8
Simchat Torah, 32
sin, 9, 31, 32
skatole, 36
skin, 4, 38, 84–85
skull, 40, 44
slaughter, 3, 48–50, 69, 72, 88
smartphone, 91
smoltification, 62–63
sniffing, 18–19, 28, 43
snout, 43–44
socialization, 19, 23, 35–36, 37,
53, 66, 73, 86
soil, 38, 44, 66
Solomon, 71
sow, 17, 19, 24–25, 28, 35, 38,
42–43, 47, 55–56, 70, 84
speech, 59, 73–74
stag, 17
stall, 57–58
stockperson, 10, 35, 39, 46, 68–89
stomach, 2–3, 58–59
structure, 4, 6, 11, 14, 17, 18, 28,
29, 41, 50, 85
stunning, 3
Succoth, 32
suckling, 38–39, 83
sun, 37, 38, 63
supermarket, 91
Swona, 15
synchronization, 23–24

tail, 4, 37–39, 42, 47
tamim, 31, 33, 37, 40, 42
teat, 42–43, 52–53
teeth, 25, 42–43, 49, 58
temperature, 41, 45, 49, 63, 68, 73
temple, 32–34, 39, 70

thermoregulation, 4, 37, 41, 45, 56
tongue, 19, 44, 60
touching, 38, 81–84, 87
trade, 91
tradition, 6–7, 10–11, 13, 48–49,
50, 80, 85
trimming, 44–45
turkey, 55, 86
twins, 25–26, 46, 72, 82–83

unclean, 17, 41

vasectomy, 18, 34, 36
ventilation, 68
veterinary surgeon, 68, 88
vigilance, 21
vision, 10
vocalization, 16, 19, 21, 27, 66,
82–84
vocation, 79–80
voice, 12, 27, 73–74

wallow, 44, 55
warmth, 25, 26, 81
water, 2, 11, 46, 49, 54, 55, 62–63,
66, 70–71, 73, 77–78, 87
watering, 53, 72, 77–78, 86
waterproofing, 45, 56
weather, 2, 54, 61, 92
wedding, 21
well, 1, 77–78
wild, 3–4, 6–7, 8, 10–11, 14–15,
24–26, 35, 38, 39, 41, 44–45,
49, 52, 55, 56, 60, 61–65,
73, 74
wind, 23, 62, 63
wings, 19, 21, 27, 56, 85
woman, 43, 69, 78
work, 6, 17, 46, 68, 71, 74, 79–80

Yom Kippur, 32

Zipporah, 77
zookeeper, 79–80
zoonosis, 74

113

www.ingramcontent.com/pod-product-compliance
Lightning Source LLC
Chambersburg PA
CBHW032233080426
42735CB00008B/838